Denys Watkins-Pitchford trained as an artist and started writing under the pseudonym 'B.B.' His early books were so successful that he gave up his career as an art teacher to devote all his time to writing and illustrating. One of his books BRENDON CHASE was a successful television serial.

Manka and his first family

'B.B.'

Manka, The Sky Gipsy
The Story of a Wild Goose

Written and Illustrated by
D.J. Watkins-Pitchford

With a foreword by
Sir Peter Scott

Richard Drew Publishing
Glasgow

First published by Eyre & Spottiswoode 1939
New edition published
by Methuen Children's Books Ltd. 1970

This edition published 1988 by

Richard Drew Publishing Limited
6 Clairmont Gardens, Glasgow G3 7LW

The publisher acknowledges the assistance of the
Scottish Arts Council in the publication of this book.

British Library Cataloguing in Publication Data

'B.B.'
    Manka, the sky gipsy.
    1. Geese
    Rn: Denys James Watkins-Pitchford
    I. Title
    598.4'1

    ISBN 0-86267-222-8

Printed and bound in Great Britain by
Cox & Wyman Ltd., Reading

To My Wife

*Who has helped me in the production
of this book*

"The wonder of the world, the beauty and
the power, the shapes of things, their colours,
lights, and shades; these I saw.
Look ye also while life lasts."

FOREWORD

AS a young man in the long ago I lived in a lighthouse on the edge of a saltmarsh on the Wash. The marsh, which I first saw in 1929, was the winter haunt of some thousands of Pinkfooted Geese. At that time the call of Pinkfeet was to me the most exciting in all nature. Since then other species — Redbreasted Geese, Whitefronted Geese, and Bewick's Swans — have each laid claim to be my favourite bird, but nostalgic memories of the Wash leave the Pinkfeet in a high position.

The publication of B.B.'s "Manka" in 1939 was at the time a great thrill to me even though I had been dreaming of writing such a tale myself. The book has had a well-deserved success, and the demand for this new edition demonstrates its lasting quality.

Some of the marshes over which Manka, the sky gipsy, flew, are now no longer frequented by wild geese. The pressures of human population and development are too great. Nevertheless, the Pinkfooted Geese have maintained and even increased their numbers.

In the Foreword which I wrote for the third edition in 1969 I recorded that the Pinkfooted Geese were threatened by a proposed hydro-electric dam on the main oasis of vegetation in the central desert of Iceland, which in those days held something like half of the world's population of the species. Now 19 years later the dam still threatens, but may still not be built. And the Pinkfeet have spread their range and become much more numerous.

When this book was first published (in 1939) there were probably less than 50,000 Pinkfeet coming to the British Isles each winter. By November 1987 there were 170,000.

Meanwhile the Pinkfoot is, I think, now once more my favourite wild goose species, and watching ten thousand of them tumbling in to roost on Martin Mere is for me the pinnacle of wildlife experiences in Britain.

Peter Scott

Slimbridge
1988

Chapter One
THE WATERFALL

The heavy water, eternally falling over the sill, descended in a thick sheet into a cauldron fifty feet below, taking with it air-bubbles that rose again below the thresh of waters in swelling, dirty-white mushrooms, that furled and broke in spinning suck-pools and foam-clots.

THE dull booming thunder of the fall was a constant sound.

Even when mighty, full-voiced winds came rushing through Brent Pass and down the Esker valley, the roar was still there, fainter as the wind caught it, then loud again, as if the ears had been stopped for a moment by an inserted finger.

The river was thick and muddy with snow water, for all the surrounding ice-fields drained into the valley, sending a multitude of silver gutters downwards that grew in size and volume with each foot of their descent. Seen from the high ground above the Esker these countless tributaries appeared like the veins in a withered oak leaf.

Southwards, above the waterfall, wide ice-fields rose to meet the sky, clean and spotless as a newly starched tablecloth.

Anyone standing above the waterfall and looking North would have seen the high peak of Temple Mountain rearing into the clouds and, across the Sassendal river—the main river into which the waterfall ultimately delivered its flood—the Colorado hills forming a wall of deepest indigo, streaked and patched with snow that shone with a weird vividness against the sombre colours of the rock.

The heavy water, eternally falling over the sill, descended in a thick sheet to the cauldron fifty feet below, taking with it air-bubbles that rose again below the thresh of waters in swelling dirty-white

3

mushrooms that furled and broke in spinning suck-pools and foam-clots.

Sometimes blocks of ice came over, rearing for an instant on the edge, then turning, flashing blindingly if the sun was shining, to fall down into the turmoil beneath.

Below the fall the carboniferous limestone had been chiselled and rounded into sharp bluffs, or more properly, miniature cliffs that stood vertically in the river flood. And as the river debouched among the bogs that fringed the Sassendal, these bluffs sank into the ground. Higher up the river valley there were few flowers, but here, where the rocks gave way to the spongy ground streaked with emerald mosses, all manner of brilliant plants blossomed. Most vivid of all were the carpets of saxifrage, growing on the drier ground, and the delicate petals of the Arctic poppy, and little potentillas.

But it is the immediate vicinity of the fall that concerns us, for it was here Manka's first impressions of the world were registered, and it is important to have the picture firmly in the mind.

It was not a large river. Below the fall and before it broadened out beyond the low limestone bluffs, it was not more than nine yards across.

The current was swift, pent up between the unyielding walls, and now, at the height of the Arctic summer, the maximum weight of water was coming down over the fall.

In a land of silence the sound of it was comforting, and for thousands and thousands of years it had gone on, dying each winter in the grip of the frost, but never really dead, only muffled beneath a fairy roof of ice. All through the Arctic winter this region was fantastic and terrible, truly awful in its loneliness, as dreadful to contemplate as the forgotten or dimly imagined depths of the deepest seas.

Here was a world in the making, and it was as if the Creator had made a mess of things. The mountains, the rocks and glaciers, seemed left in a half-constructed state, something begun and never finished; as though even the Creator had given up in despair and gone away.

But on this Arctic midnight, when the story of Manka has its first beginnings, it was a world of strange and dreamlike beauty.

The low red sun, swollen to terrifying dimensions like a harvest moon seen through mist, swam slowly behind the crest of Grit Ridge, passing behind the snowy peak of far Mount Lusitania, seeming almost to bounce, like a child's gigantic ball, or an inflated balloon, from peak to peak and from ice-field to glacier.

Seventy yards below the fall, opposite a low limestone bluff that held against the opaque current like the battering-ram of an ancient ship, a reindeer's horn was lying on the stones, close to the water's edge.

It resembled a broken branch that had been carried down by the current and tossed up upon the shore. It had lain there for three whole winters and its original owner was far away beyond Wiche Bay, his shadow long in the low midnight sun.

On one of the topmost tines a small bird was perched, feeling among its breast feathers. It was a snow-bunting, the only animated thing, besides the water, in that weird and lonely valley. The force of the current piling against the ram varied in height, now dropping almost as much as a foot, now surging again as it battled and lost with the unyielding stone.

Something fell from the cliff above. It was a lightsome thing, of feather lightness, and the current gripped it and whirled it off down-river, rushing it headlong between the rocks, now floating it gently along a smooth reach, but always bearing it onwards towards the Sassendal. Once it caught between two rocks and even that frail thing held for a moment against the push of the current, then lingeringly let go and was swept onwards.

A big glaucous gull, beating over the mosses, saw it and stooped, taking it skilfully from the water with forward wagging wing and downhung paddles.

But he dropped it again into the stream and it floated on and was lost among the mosses. Soon it reappeared where the Esker river joined the Sassendal and where a swifter eddy caught it and turned it sideways, it filled and slowly sank, rocking down into the muddy depths.

It was part of an egg-shell, that for three weeks had been a gosling's prison.

In the depths of the Arctic night, when the sun had gone, and left this world to get along as best as it could until he should come again, the fall was a magnificent spectacle; never a human eye had seen it then.

Each ledge of overhanging rock held a column of fluted ice, like organ-pipes, or the stalactites and stalagmites of a fairy cave.

But now it was in half shadow and free of ice, only the top of the fall was visible and there was a reddish light cast upon the bluffs.

Sitting on one of the narrow ledges thirty feet above the river was a brooding pink-footed goose. She seemed a bird of dreams in a land of dreams, completely incongruous and out of keeping.

Her place was surely among the bogs at the mouth of the river, not here, perched on a ledge of naked limestone like a falcon or a raven. From time to time she turned her head, creasing her long and sinuous neck, listening to the music of the water as it thundered, now muffled, now loud, over the fall. She had heard the keening of a glaucous gull somewhere down-river, the sharp sound had cut across the roar of waters. But reassured, her head sank back upon her shoulders and she became part of the rock itself.

On other ledges above her and below were other brooding geese, each with the mate on guard beside them, for there was a colony of thirty birds nesting by the waterfall.

When the sun came over a distant ridge like a big red crown, she rose slowly and twisted her snake-like neck sideways to watch her precious eggs. For some time she had felt dull knockings inside the smooth thick shells and even muffled peepings that seemed to come out of the depths of the ledge.

A gosling was breaking from its prison, struggling with blind movements as dreadful as death throes, the same blind forces that drive the spike of the bulb through the hard earth or that split the case of the chrysalis.

Now and again it rested from its labours, its little back heaving in exhaustion, and then, with a last violent motion, it split the shell and the two halves fell apart.

After a rest it crept from the bloodstained shell into the warmth and dryness of its mother's thighs.

The goose took the half of empty shell and tweaked it over the ledge, the other half rolled into a crevice and was crushed by the goose's paddle. Feeble peepings were redoubled, the other eggs were hatching, and at the end of two hours, when the sun was clear of the ridge and flooded the chasm with wan light, all had hatched. Snow came wandering, thickening as the clouds obscured the sun, and the flakes settled upon the broad grey back of the mother, melting into little beads.

Now the snow quickly passed and the sky blazed with colour. A path of gold cloudlets spread fanwise in the sky against pale lapis lazuli, and these wondrous colours were reflected in a little lake among the bogs below the fall. Two whooper swans, rare stragglers to this lone isle, sat there motionless, grey against ice⁄blue, their long necks as stiff as pokers. Miraculously they began to move as gracefully and as slowly as liners leaving dock, clucking wild musical notes one to another. On an impulse they leant forward on the water, threshing the colours of the sky into a mess, like a broken stained⁄glass window.

Their wide wings spread and their necks nodded with the exertion of rising from the surface. Hompa! hompa! hompa! Their reflections slid with them, drops of water fell from the down⁄hung black paddles and made little fairy rings on the colourful mirror. Lifting across the dark bogs, they wheeled towards the sun, dissolving like vapour against its glare. One moment they told blue against a distant dark rock face, now grey as they passed a snowfield, and were gone. They had been roosting on the lake and were beginning a new day in a land of eternal day.

Slowly the surface of the lake became again as glass and a wee white breast feather drifted to the shore, a fairy boat on a fairy lake. It came to rest against the stones, turning now this way now that as the breeze eddies caught it.

And then the picture in the mirror changed. The lapis lazuli faded to give way to palest daffodil and the trident peaks to the south were the colour of a bee-heavy wallflower in an English garden. Still the colours changed, the velvet-red of the peaks to deepest indigo and the path of gold cloudlets dissolved away in wisps of vapour. Three shadows ran along the margin of the lake. They were the reflections of three purple sandpipers that were hunting the muds, probing delicately with their fine bills.

A big grey bullet came singing from the dawn sky and the sandpipers scattered in alarm with shrill cries. One darted into the mosses, another up a gully, and the third flickered across the lake.

The big falcon came down in a long stoop, struck, and swept up again into the sky. A tiny spot fell apart from the little bird, its body falling with a splash; the spot was the sandpiper's head, and began to drift away towards the mosses.

The mother goose on the ledge stood up carefully, feeling with tender deliberation among her rocking unsteady goslings that peeped with renewed frenzy beneath her.

These tiny mites, what had the future in store for them? Would those absurd little flippers ever grow into wide wings, strong enough to bear them to far wild lands? Surely not, it seemed fantastic!

For all her seeming care the mother put one of her paddles on a gosling, which peeped in urgent agony. She drew her foot quickly into her flank and put it down again, feeling for the hard rock. With graceful tread she walked to the edge of the bluff, looking towards the waterfall and the distant windings of the river as it melted into the bogs.

The colours had faded from the sky and thick clouds hid the high ice-fields. Behind her the four babies snuggled together, tucking their little pudgy bills under one another's flippers and shivering with cold.

Melting snow dripped off a cornice and fell pat! on to a ledge below. Pat! Pat! A wind rose and ruffled the feathers of the vigilant mother. A goose flew up the chasm and the mother goose called to it, for it was her mate.

He banked round and landed on the ledge beside her. As though to display her family, she led him back to the nest, pausing a moment before settling down on them and fluffing out her feathers.

The proud gander stood a long time close to the nest and then began pacing to and fro along the ledge of the rocks as though he were on sentry-go. For many days he had done this. Wild geese are devoted parents and guard their goslings jealously. Well they have need to, for in that land of cliff and glacier, skuas, glaucous gulls, and Arctic foxes, are a constant source of danger to both eggs and young.

The four little goslings were clad in greenish down, each with a patch of olive green on the back of the head, yellow flanks and tummies, and olive lores behind the eyes. The only difference visible in Manka was the colour of the eye. In the other goslings this was dark, but in Manka it was almost white, or rather a milky pink which gave him rather a blind look. His sight was as good as his brothers and sisters, however.

There was a continuous procession of gulls, fulmars, skuas, and kittiwakes, passing over the cliffs. They bred in countless thousands in the loomeries on the coast, and the wicked glaucous and skuas were always hunting the valleys inland for fledglings and eggs. But they saw the big gander standing guard on the bluffs and passed on, turning their wicked eyes sideways and downwards, screaming derisively as they scanned the nesting ledges. Sometimes they found an unguarded nest of eggs or young, but the geese were ever on the watch, and sometimes the ganders went up aloft and mobbed them. Many had young of their own to feed, so it was all in life's game.

When the mother goose raised herself on the nest, the light and cold caused an outburst of peeping from the goslings as they burrowed their heads under one another's flippers. It was then Manka heard the dull thunder of the fall for the first time, a sound he was to remember to his life's end.

There was a ryper calling from a rock on the other side of the stream. It was higher up the cliffs, standing on a snow patch, a large bird with claws as strong as eagle's claws and a brown mottled plumage, a bigger bird than the Scottish ptarmigan. It was brown-spotted now, but later it would turn snow-white. "Bec! bec! bec!" . . . the sound cut across the drum of the waterfall. Its mate was sitting on a nest up above the snow patch.

The gander watched suspiciously and whenever a bird, gull, or goose, passed up the river below the ledge, he craned his head over and watched its passage. The brooding goose did likewise.

The rock had been worn quite smooth and shiny by the constant friction of the gander's paddles. He had mounted guard over many families on the ledge and he knew the ways of glaucous and skua. No fox could reach them here, for it was well below the top of the cliff, and though foxes often came along the edge and peered over with their cunning slits of eyes, they dared not jump down on to the narrow ledge. Other nests close to the fall were robbed by foxes every year, for they were easy of access, yet the younger geese, who were inexperienced, built there each summer.

A thick mist came in from the bay, hiding the bluffs and blanketing the ice-fields and the marshes by the Sassendal. The "bec! bec!" of the ryper still sounded from the hill, but it was now invisible and a distant mountain fired a salute of stones and rocks that had been loosened by the thaw. The sound rumbled and echoed from peak to peak and valley to valley, dying away in faint murmurs muffled by the fog.

The gander jumped from the ledge. In an instant the mist swallowed him and a quietness and dampness settled down. Sometimes there was a swish of invisible wings passing over head, some gull or skua or a wandering goose. Even the roar of the fall seemed subdued, and so thick was the mist that it hid the opposite rock face. The goose heard the monotonous talk of the river below and far away the clamour of gulls on the main river. Her neck was sunk in her shoulders and her eyes almost closed. Beneath her she felt the warm little bodies burrowing and peeping between her thighs and she was content.

Then the chatter of the water altered in tone, a dislodged rock splashed down, and there was a sound of grunting and sloshing, of bony feet clattering on the stones. Something was crossing the river farther down, but the mist was so thick the goose could see nothing. Her neck was very straight now and she turned her head all ways and craned it, snake-like, over the ledge, but all she saw was the brown crinkling water running to the sea. Whatever the beast was it went up-river a little way and then clattered up the rocks towards the higher ground. After a while the sounds died away. But the ryper, who up to now had been calling his "bec! bec!" at intervals, fell silent and the goose heard the whirr of his wings as he left the snow-slope and a sudden outburst of explosive "becs!"

Perhaps it was a reindeer or possibly a bear, though the latter rarely came as far as the Esker valley.

As soon as the goslings had been dry some hours the next business was to get them away from the ledge.

Now they were hatched there was the ever-present danger of the cruel gulls, and on the ledge they were without cover of any sort. The gulls, seeming to sense in some curious way that the goslings were going to leave the nest, came flickering through the fog, wheeling round and up and down between the bluffs. But while they patrolled the stream the mother goose sat tight, keeping her babies beneath her while the hissing gander mounted guard, stretching his neck at each stooping gull that swept past the ledge.

At last the robbers wearied of waiting and went away over the fall to look for the ptarmigan's nest among the stones. Now was the chance. Both geese flopped into the water, calling to their babies to follow. For a moment they hung back, running up and down the ledge in a peeping group. Manka, peering over, could see nothing but a misty void, with now and again the dim form of the goose or gander swimming off the main race of the current.

Then Manka went over, flippers spread and paddles wide, peeping in terror as the air let him fall. After him came the other goslings in a shower, each alighting on the water like corks. Nameless forces gripped Manka, the eddies span him round, but his little paddles kicked skilfully as though he had swum for weeks, different indeed from the naked helpless atoms that were the snow-buntings' babies, in the cranny of a rock above the snow-field.

It was only a few yards to a rocky promontory and the current bore him thither, smoothly and surely, his tiny paddles felt stones beneath him and together with the other scared babies they scrambled out. A moment later the whole brood was running with surprising swiftness among the boulders, the goose in front and the gander bringing up the rear, as advance guard and rearguard.

Perhaps the most dangerous time in the whole of Manka's life was when the family began this trek to the lake.

The goose went before, picking her way carefully between the stones and over the sticky muds with her peeping babies scrambling after. They had to keep a weather eye open for the cruel freebooters of the sky, but the two adult geese were ever on the watch. It was a journey of five hundred yards from the river to the lake and every step of the way was fraught with peril. It was like some dreadful game of chance, not unmixed with skill, for the glaucous had to be quick to seize a gosling and be away before the more clumsy geese could come to the rescue. They had not gone many yards from the bluffs before a glaucous, sailing on outspread wings across a far snow-field, saw the little family party making their way over the ground.

It came down in one big swoop with down-dropped paddles. But the gander was there. He ran forward with closed wings, his beak wide open and looking very fierce.

Up soared the gull with a twist of its pinions and the mother goose had called the babies beneath her and sat crouched between the cushions of herbage on the bare cracked ground. These cracks were everywhere. They were not due to heat but the shrinkage of the earth after the fierce frosts of winter. Frost and the laws of gravitation were slowly pulling the mountains down, and the ground about their bases was a mass of porridge, mud, stones, glaciers, and snow bogs.

And on this flat ground there were curious bosses or nodules of mud, also due to the contracting of the ground. Some of the cracks were miniature crevasses in which a walking-stick might be lost.

Dark death, beating in the thrilling vanes of the swooping gulls and skuas, also lurked among this tumbled rough ground.

One of the little goslings, which thought himself left behind, ran peeping wildly to catch up with his mother. In his hurry he slipped and fell, just as a human baby falls, and the downy body tumbled, paddles up, into one of the crevasses. The fissure was only six inches deep, but it was half an inch wider than the gosling, and there he lay, jammed in the bottom of the crack. The procession came to a halt, something had gone wrong. Muffled peeps seemed to come out of the ground and the parent geese were nonplussed. They had not the sense to know that one of their babies was down the crack. Uneasily the goose and gander scanned the surrounding herbage, but they only saw the nodding yellow poppy-heads blowing in the wind and the red carpets of saxifrage and the caked, cracked earth. And so they went on towards the lake. Down in the crevasse two little paddles worked to and fro, like the toys one sees on the London pavements. The gosling was jammed tight and could not turn over, even had he been able to he would not have got out. He made frantic efforts to right himself, for he could see the clear sky and the nodding head of a poppy. But it was all to no purpose.

The tiny legs kicked more slowly as though the springs were running down. One leg stopped, then started again, one two, one two . . . one . . . two . . . one . . . two. It stopped. The squeaks became feebler then ceased also, for it was a very tired little gosling and this life business was not a nice affair. . . . Perhaps its bones, no bigger than a mouse's bones, still lie in that crack in far Spitzbergen. Many winters have passed since that day the goose family journeyed to the pool. Snow has come and covered the fissure and all has been darkness and cold. A fox's nose snuffled at the crack, but only a tiny trickle of dry dust came down. And the reindeer's horn by the waterfall has long since rotted away.

Chapter Two
SPITZBERGEN

O' nights now there was a strange, darting, white glare over North East Land. This was the ice blink over the solid ice which every day moved nearer and nearer with the sureness of an advancing tide. Strange boomings and grindings came from the sea as of a giant, that muttered and ground his teeth.

THE arctic summer is so short, it is necessary that birds bred in those regions of ice and snow should develop rapidly.

It was now late July and in little more than eight weeks time the geese must be on their way South.

The three remaining goslings had, in a few perilous weeks, doubled their size. Their quills were sprouting. Manka's feathers, bursting like folded leaves from split bud casings, were white. He was a strange object, speckled all over his breast and back with white. His wings were white, whilst those of his companions were a soft grey. They could not fly as yet, but ran, like young partridge cheepers, with their parents. For ten days or so the latter were also deprived of the powers of flight (before the new feathers grew), all ran with surprising ease and speed for such large birds.

Wild geese have long legs and in this respect differ from the domesticated goose. When alarmed the goslings spread their wings wide whilst running, but their parents kept theirs closed and so had greater speed.

The blossoms on the mosses faded. No more did the red saxifrages carpet the ground, the frail white flowers upon the slopes were now withered seed-pods, and Arctic poppies no longer waved at each passing breath. The marshes were of a darker, richer hue than at early summer, thereby accentuating the dazzling white of snow-field and glacier. Mists became more frequent, thick walls of white opaqueness that came in from the sea whence the far clashings of ice were faintly audible.

Manka and his two sisters began to make efforts to fly, and their parents encouraged them, for the latter soon grew new flight feathers and knew again the ease and freedom of the air. They sprang from hummock to hummock with clumsy wing beats, falling over in their efforts at landing, but all the time becoming more skilful in their management and mastery of flight. Each day they felt more keenly the bondage of the earth, and with something allied to human envy, watched the wheeling gulls and full-grown geese flying about the deep-toned marshes around Sassen Bay. The graceful Arctic terns (that bred among the stony foreshore in Advent Bay) mocked their clumsy efforts, hovering like little white hawks above the goslings flopping among the mosses.

One memorable morning Manka took his first real flight.

A big falcon, soaring over the marshes, saw the three goslings among the rough tussocks close to the lake and stooped at them. It was only in play, for a falcon's habit is to take his prey on the wing, but the terrified goslings scattered, flapping and flopping in every direction. Manka jumped upwards and found himself flying. For the first time the air bore him up, and though at first he flapped frantically when he found himself sinking, he soon found that, like a swimmer in water, if he took slower and more measured strokes he kept up without trouble. It was a marvellous sensation, and he gloried in it. If an animal or bird can feel exultant surely Manka did at that moment as he swept across the little lake and saw the ripples passing so quickly beneath his down-dropped paddles. In a matter of seconds he was over the bright water and crossing the marsh on the other side, heading in a steep bank that nearly brought disaster, for the broad ribbon of the Sassendal.

Still he kept up, noting the boulders and the bogs passing so rapidly beneath him until, exhausted, he lifted his wings and let himself sink downwards into a carpet of deep green moss. Quickly his wings folded, apparently of themselves, and he shook out his tail and looked about him. There was no sign of the falcon, for it had passed on, but the sky was full of gulls and terns and out beyond an ice floe, three long-tailed ducks swam buoyantly, like exotic pheasants with their long tails cocked out behind.

Resting on a mud bar were geese, some young like himself, others old birds whose new flights had not been sprouted a week, all standing in a long line like a rank of soldiers at drill.

After this he took flights every day, always increasing his powers and understanding, and learning the security of the invisible airs. The glaucous left him alone now and did not even mob him as they did the other goslings, possibly because he was white like themselves, and they thought he was a new and formidable species of gull.

Wonderful sunsets were reflected in the lake, and for three days in mid-August the sun shone all day (as well as night) from a sky of deepest blue. On the third day a lumbering barrel of a reindeer came sloshing through the marsh, with many belly rumblings and constantly flapping ears, for the midges were torturing him. Manka saw him and was afraid, running at first and then lying down with outstretched neck. This is a curious habit of wild geese, and even the adult birds adopted the same attitude when badly frightened.

But the great beast took no heed of the white goose, he passed up a wild corrie where mighty ice blocks were scattered. He was making for the high ground where the midges ceased from troubling and where others of his kind were to be found.

And then came the time when the sun was hidden behind the blue ice-fields for an hour or more at midnight, and the whole world became wrapt in an unearthly twilight. Then a sombre cloak was drawn about the hills that lingered long in the valleys where mists smoked whitely. The summer was drawing to its end, and soon the life-giving heat and life would be hidden for four long months.

One afternoon Manka flew up to the waterfall and over the

bluffs. The sound of the fall was familiar, dearly so, but there were no geese on the ledges, even the down had blown away from the nesting hollows. The place was utterly deserted. Manka came to rest close to the fall, and hunted along the edge of the river for tender grass shoots. He passed the reindeer's horn, but there was no little stumpy bunting singing on its tines, only a spot or two of white lime on the grey stone beneath. And feeling suddenly the loneliness of the place, he took wing again, and the murmur of the fall dwindled behind him. He went back to the marshes and found his companions there, washing and playing in the shallows of the lake.

O' nights now there was a strange, darting, white glare over North East Land. This was the ice blink over the solid ice which every day moved nearer and nearer with the sureness of the advancing tide. One morning the bay was partly frozen with a skin of ice, and only the inland pools remained open. Strange boomings and grindings came from the sea, as of a giant that muttered and ground his teeth.

The geese grew more and more restless. At first they felt a faint uneasiness, roused perhaps by the sight and sound of high-flying Brent geese, or even the whisper of Fulmar wings, for there was a daily procession of these birds on passage, all bound in the same direction. And then this uneasiness became a pain which was part of the waking and sleeping life of Manka. Together with other geese, he took long flights over the sea beyond Advent and Wiche Bays, returning in the evenings to the Sassendal, where he roosted with over a hundred other geese, out on the mud bars. More and more geese swelled their ranks, and by the middle of September over a thousand geese had congregated in Sassen Bay.

Out on a lonely point was a ruined wooden hut, relic of some Dutch whalers that had wintered there over a generation before Manka was born. They had been trapped by the savage stealthy ice, and never lived to see the sun again. The rotting timbers had been swollen by the rains and contracted by the frosts, the roof gaped. And down in the black mosses of the foreshore were other remains; a rusty anchor, the broken haft of a harpoon and some Dutch coins.

Farther along the shore there was a wooden cross, still standing, dreadful in its isolation, and an oblong box with the lid missing. Staring at the sky was a sightless skull, and ribs and bones lay scattered about, where bears and foxes had played with them. Many an arctic night had those sightless sockets stared to heaven, watching, so it seemed, the moving colour-curtains of the Northern lights. Those waving curtains seemed sometimes as if they were about to part, to reveal the Creator of all things come to beckon the dead to a resurrection. One could imagine the bones gathering themselves together; the flesh (that once covered them) forming about the naked framework, at first as a mist, and then with solid curve and contour, and the bearded hunter, in his outlandish clothes, stepping over the side of the box and falling to his knees.

Manka sometimes came to this lonely point, but the hut aroused suspicion in his mind, and he gave it a wide berth. In some curious way it smelt of danger, though he knew not why. And when he was here, one misty day, something loomed out of the fog close inshore.

A fairy castle in peacock blues and greens, with postern doors and battlemented keeps, and fairy buttresses and embrasures. But no figures manned the ramparts, it drifted silently as though propelled by invisible engines, slowly, slowly past the point, to be swallowed in the mist.

Beyond a honk of alarm, Manka did not move. He stood, a white figure, watching the iceberg dissolve into the fog.

At the beginning of September, more ice appeared in Sassen Bay, and at night the white gleam to the North grew brighter. The pack ice was now only a few miles North, and soon the island would be gripped solid until the spring.

Now the pain grew so strong the geese could hardly rest. They flew in small parties hither and thither, lining the banks in their grey regiments (the white spot of Manka appearing very conspicuous by comparison) awaiting some secret signal we can only dimly comprehend. Humans at times have a faint ghost of this restlessness that the geese felt, that longing to be gone from the old familiar places to seek strange new lands. As we become more civilized we feel this instinct less and less, we become more akin to the machines that govern our little lives.

To the geese it was a call that must be obeyed, as strong as life itself. The South drew them as a magnetic pole draws the needle.

The snow came to whiten the marshes, and Manka, flying over the waterfall, bound for Brent Pass, saw bearded icicles shielding the curtain of water that ran clearer now than at any time since the spring. Only the tip of the reindeer's horn peeped above a new-fallen mantle of snow that was spread upon the rocks. A large, yellowish-white object was ambling above the bluffs, a polar bear. Manka was so interested he wheeled about, croaking in alarm. But the bear took no heed, and finally disappeared among the tumbled blocks of ice.

Low clouds hid the cliffs, trailing in fantastic shapes and whirling a ghostly dance about the glaciers, sometimes assuming the forms of giant men and women, fantastic monsters and horned devils. Everywhere there was sense of the lights being turned down; the play was over, and the curtain fast falling. There was a sense too, of preparation. Preparation for what: for the dark months when only the stars and moon gave fitful light, or when the Northern Lights played upon the ice and frozen plain that was once open sea? For the time when all the birds had gone, when the loomeries on the cliffs were silent, and only the foxes, reindeer, and bears, were left to face the winter through? So must have the world appeared before it was alive, alive with the sunlight and flicker of white wings.

Already the gulls had left the cliffs, the shrieking bustle of auks, puffins, and skuas, had gone. Only the grim sea, doomed to eternal battling with the rocks, boomed and sucked among the ice caverns, or ran its grey ram against the snout of the glaciers. The little purple sandpipers had fled, and no longer did the eider fleets ride the waves within the bay. They were out at sea, among the big green rollers that were playing quoits with numberless little ice floes. In Sassen Bay the sea was oily-still, for Northwards there was a firm-locked barrier that broke all wind and swell. A stilling of everything; of bird voices, of the homely wash of waves along the shore where the terns and sandpipers had nested, a silencing of rivers and streams, of all the laughter of the sun.

Yet still the geese lingered, wings must be strong for the long journey that lay before. Night after night, however, little parties slipped away. Next morning there were fewer geese ranged along the bars. Manka's parents, unable to bear the pain longer, left with thirty other geese. Their youngsters remained in company with sixty or more others, who still waited for the strength and courage to depart.

Only for a few hours did the sun shine, sometimes not at all when the clouds were low. The sea froze solid in Sassen Bay. For the last time Manka flew up to the fall, with his two sisters, and the voice of the fall was muted by ice pillars as thick round as forest oaks. Snow lay in white bands along the bluffs (the ledge where he was hatched was two feet under) and the reindeer's horn was hidden and would not appear again until the following spring.

Dusky Brent geese, white collared and royal, passed, all one day, high and bugling in compact arrowheads and chevrons, half hidden by low, driving cloud. On top of the ruined hut, the snow was deep, and the lidless coffin had a drift that nearly covered it, the bones had a new winding-sheet. Some animal had taken the skull from the coffin and carried it up the shore. Winds, snow-charged and stinging, raced across the barrens, and then, one night, it ceased to blow.

A fearful silence fell, the sea was mastered at last, no more thundering avalanches startled the quiet of night. The frost had also gripped the elusive streams as an otter grips a slithery trout. Only the red sun moved for a short space above the hills at noon.

The pain, the wild pain that the geese know, was no longer to be borne. Manka, together with fifteen other geese, mostly young of the year like himself, rose for the last time above the Sassendal that lay like a white band upon the dark marsh, and turned South. Whither they were bound they knew not, they had no chart or compass to guide them on their way. Clamouring one to another they wheeled upwards in a vast spiral until the river was a mere thread below and Sassen Bay no larger than a sixpence. They saw the greater part of the island at a glance, and North, the white plain of ice that stretched to the Pole.

Then, with a sudden wild crying that echoed among their ranks, they fell into station, each astern of the other, and wing beats began a deathless tattoo. Flying in so much disturbed air was new to Manka. In addition to the "whoof" "whoof" of thirty-two wings all beating in unison, he felt the rush of air past his lores as his bill cleft the sticky air asunder, the suctional pull behind the forward camber of his wings. Higher and yet higher rose the skein, falling into the formation of a big arrowhead, an arrow that pointed to the South, that slowly dwindled beyond the far mountain peaks.

It seemed then that darkness and silence took immediate command. The geese had been the vanguard of the retreating army. Northwards the ice-blink quivered and jumped, not a bird called or a wing beat in all that silent land about Sassen Bay. By the hut on Starvation Point the sightless skull stared upwards, two cavern-ous spots of shadow with snow for eyes. It could not see the black arrowhead of geese pass over against the stars. No longer did the ice groan and crash out in the bay, or fairy bergs come drifting through the mist. The land was forgotten again and was ready for its long sleep. And somewhere out in Sassen Bay, far below the roof of ice that now stretched for hundreds of miles to the Pole, a

Sassen Bay

half of an egg-shell lay between two rocks. The bright spirit that had once been its tenant was now beating Southwards towards Bear Island, crying the wild cry that tells of the great pain.

Behind, Spitzbergen lay like a little white cloud sitting on the ocean, ahead there was nothing but the dark curve of the seas' horizon. Beneath them were scattered white lumps, of all sizes, so that the sea appeared not unlike Hampstead Heath after a bank holiday. Soon these white lumps (which were ice floes) became less frequent until there was nothing but faint streaks that came and went as the crests of the waves broke downwards into the billows.

Far below, little man-ships toiled along, leaving a smear across the dark plain of the sea as a snail leaves a trail behind it. They toiled so slowly, and with so much labour, across the grey continents of water that the ease of the speeding arrowheads of birds seemed to mock them. Half naked men, down in the white tanks of engine rooms sweated and laboured among the thrusting pistons, surrounded by a network of steel in an atmosphere sickly with oil. And they knew nothing of the geese passing over. Rusty old tramps, their bows white under in the swell; brilliant liners, lit from stem to stern, where in palm-decked ballrooms people danced and made believe they were still on land; all passed under, none knew or cared about the geese. Little atoms of life, puppets drawn by the strings of circumstance, all weaving and interweaving, as changeful as the sea. High above, their heads in the stars, the geese drove onwards in a black arrowhead, elemental as the land they had left behind them. By dawn they had passed Bear Island, soon Iceland lay to the West, but they turned not aside.

Manka was glorying in the power of flight. A beautiful bird, like something out of Hans Andersen's fairy tales, as white as a Spitzbergen snow-field, the very embodiment of all that is wild and free, intense with vivid life.

His wings moved rhythmically, responding to every air current, the shaped flight feathers, on which stability depended, spreading like fingers with every downward thrust, closing again as he raised his wings. He rose to the invisible billows as a ship rises to the swell, he sank again into the troughs of air, always steady, always in command of the yielding substance.

To fall, he would have to close his wings and drop his head, as a swimmer in water, but now the air held his quill feathers open like a kite. With every downthrust he rose upwards, sinking gently as his wings finished their sweep. It was circular motion; up (to take hold of the air), round and back and down; up, round, back, and down; up, round, back, and down; his wings a screw that drove him forwards.

Each goose flew in the slipstream of the next ahead at a speed somewhere about ninety miles per hour. Ahead of Manka were eight other geese; the leader was an old bird that had seen twelve Spitzbergen summers. He weighed six and a half pounds. The last summer had been a tragic one for him. He had lost his mate and four goslings to an arctic fox, so he had lingered. But now his sorrow was forgotten in the great pain. As they flew, goose answered goose, the sound rippled down the ranks in a wave of bugle notes. The sky was full of other birds, fleeing before the cold, skein after skein of geese were passing over the grey plain of the sea far below, all flying at an altitude of over ten thousand feet. Now massed banks of vapour appeared below them, solid in appearance as land, Manka was tempted to drop his paddles and alight among the snowy cushions. Now and again, though a ragged, black hole, the sea could be glimpsed, with the surface crinkled and creased like corrugated paper. Then for a space the woolly white blankets dissolved away and the geese sped on in a moonlit world of un-reality, darkness below and darkness above, the glitter of the moon on the sea, star dust above them. Then cloud again, a steady blanket. They rose to clear it, but even after their strong wings had borne them seven hundred feet higher, they were soon flying in a dense cloud bank that obscured everything. It was so cold that tiny particles of ice began to form on the vanes of their tails and on the back camber of their wings. On the left, the mist grew lighter and soon came the sun again; they saw the round, bright globe before the ships could see it. "Woof" "woof" "woof" in a gladsome concert the strong pinions sang the flight song, the wind song of the free skyroads. Manka's feet were tucked up out of sight like the retractable landing gear of modern flying machines, he felt the suctional pull behind his shoulders, the pull that held him up, and the soft, icy stream of air flowing along his flanks and sliding off his outer tail coverts. That glorious rush through the dawn air, how can it be described? There was that sense of speed that the airman in his modern enclosed cockpit never feels, the surge of his body forward with every powerful stroke. Like a bullet with wings, or an arrow shaft with thrilling vanes, the swish, the drive, the speed! South! South! South! "Here!" called a goose. "Where?" answered another. "Here!" called the leader, as he drove at the head of the skein. Whistle of wind, thrum of vanes, effortless motion, effortless speed! Paling stars and warmer air. Dainty wisps of cloud, like veils, passed under their paddles, one moment ahead, another moment they had flashed by; those fleeting wisps of vapour and the streaming wind gave the true sense of speed.

Behind lay the darkness, the cold, the land that was unfinished, ahead lay the warm South and fat fare, a green land of gentler airs, well loved, well known. Beneath them at last, through a rent in the clouds, they saw the Shetland islands, ringed about with white foam, land at last after so long! But they did not set their wings and glide to earth, the journey was far from finished. They saw the angry white of the rollers about Cape Wrath, the bare, bleak hills where wee, white farms crouched to be out of unceasing winds, tapes of roads where specks passed to and fro, valleys, pine clad, and snow capped mountains. And there was new light now, not the feeble glare of a weary sun, but vivid, sunpatched hillsides, tawny with bracken, rushing rivers (once, three stags fording a torrent) cloud shadows patching a long, stony hillside. The geese lowered now, when they saw the land, but still they were high. Their shadows sped with them like fairy sheep, up hill and down valley; purple woods they saw, and the blue reek from a lodge chimney, belts of dark firs, the sweet trees that were new things to Manka. Then the white ribbon of the Tay and the reek of towns. But still they did not alter course though the sun was westering, turning the hills red and casting great blue shadows where detail was drowned, as the bed of a stream is lost in deep water. They passed high over Holy Island (where the houses were beginning to light their lamps) and long lines of white rollers beat ceaselessly upon the wide sands by Bamburgh.

Still the leader led them on. Manka was tired. He would have liked to let himself sink down and rest on those firm sands, yet still the pain was not spent and he must obey, he must yet beat on, the journey was nearly done.

Then came the Humber with big ships plying, bell buoys and lightships. For over fifteen hundred miles Manka's wings had beat, now only a few hundred miles remained.

The sun eluded them in his eternal race, darkness was falling and the world below was muffled, starred with lamps and bright with furnace glares. From the mastheads of ships sprang little points of light.

Quite suddenly Manka felt the pain was at an end. The wings of the leader ceased to beat, and calling one to another they lowered, throwing themselves downwards through the air with closed wings, "tumbling" in all directions. They passed a bell in a cage that clanged wildly in the passing wash of a steamer. At first the sound was faint, then loud as they swept past it, "clang! clang! CLANG! clang! . . ." it died behind them. Round they wheeled, still calling, and Manka saw solid sand beneath, not a foot from his paddles; shells, seaweed, rocks and little pools, rushing under. He saw the grey-green herbage of the marsh and the innumerable "channers" that split up the dark expanse of sea lavender. He saw the distant blurr of the far sea wall and flocks of little silver dunlin rushing along the water edge.

The tide was running out and the sandbanks were exposed. Down on to a bar the geese descended in a grey cloud, wings lifted for the last time as each goose stalled to a standstill, folding wings across tired backs.

The air was so much warmer and softer, the birds noticed this at once, and there was no rush of icy wind past them. Instead of the "swoosh, swoosh" of wings there was the rustle of the tide on the sand bars and the pipings of flighting waders, curlews, redshanks, and golden plover.

From the land came the smell of good, moist earth, farms and woods.

After the long journey the geese were dead weary and no sentries were posted. In a moment or two each goose had tucked in his head. Some drew up one leg, most sat down on the sand and went sound asleep. So much had happened in the last few hours, there was a sense now of overwhelming peace and quietness. Manka's wings ached and his neck was weary. As soon as his eyes were shut he surely must have dreamt of the weary pilgrimage that was now at an end, of the waterfall, the glaciers, of the ruined hut on Starvation Point.

A dull throbbing pulsed through his dreams and became part of them. A steamer was going up the Wash laden with timber. The red and green of her port and starboard lights moved like coloured sparks across the dim waters and long after she had passed the dull bump of her screw persisted. Soon little white wavelets came creaming up the sand, breaking with a soft lullaby on the bar and licking the pink paddles of the sleeping geese.

All down that coast were other tired geese; some, like Manka, had come in that very night, others (including Manka's parents) had been back some days and their wings did not ache as did Manka's wings.

The first chapter of his life had been written. There was a

promise of great things to come in the talk of the misty sea and the "glug, glug" of the tide as it receded across the miles of sand.

And soon perhaps Manka did not dream, but sank down into the blessed quietude of healing sleep, heeding not when the wind, playing across the flats, ruffled his white scapulars. It was journey's end at last.

Chapter Three
THE WASH

Landwards a line of trees marked the sea-wall, bent and twisted trees that had learnt the rude breath of the sea winds; winds which seldom slept. Beyond those trees the flat Fenlands stretched, dotted with glass-houses and prosperous farms, with never a hill and scarce a wood. Ely lay beyond, a misty finger that brooded over the flat lands and reminded man there was still a God in heaven; Peterborough and Crowland, names that suggest the Viking raiders and the bitterns' boom.

THE tide was beginning to ebb, and the frothy suds and bubbles were turning again to the sea that gave them birth. At first that movement was scarcely perceptible, and it would have been hard to say whether the tide was at the ebb or flow.

Second by second the movement became more marked until there was a definite current that bore a gull's feather as fast as a cow can walk, steadily and surely, down the winding path of a creek, towards the sea.

As the water dropped inch by inch under the overhanging fringes of sea lavender, and the slimy walls of clay were laid bare, crabs sidled down from cleft and cranny, and sank into the yellow stream. They left little wavy lines on the mud that would not be washed away until the next tide. From the guts and gullies there came deep gurglings and suckings, and sometimes a wheezing noise that seemed almost a creak, as the clay clefts drained of moisture. Many stranded creatures of the sea sought frantically for water that had unaccountably fallen away beneath them and some would die before the tide brought release and life once more.

Restless pipits, whose thin cheepings were as high as bat squeaks, flitted to and fro over the grey-green marshes, and with them were snow-buntings, newly in from the far North. These birds seemed like scraps of white paper as the wind took them and tossed them this way and that, or like pale leaves that fly before October gales.

As far as the eye could see, North and South, the marshes stretched, a continuous plain of grey-green that melted into the grey of the November sky.

Nothing moved on that sombre expanse save the wiry stems of the sea lavender as the cold wind blew strongly in off the mud flats. In the distance, across the ooze, rose the targets on the Air Force ranges magnified to vast dimensions and misty with distance.

The aeroplanes had gone away, as birds migrate in autumn, and once more there was peace. Wherever man comes he brings noise, and here, on these bleak lands around the Wash, he made the air rock with the crash of gunfire and vibrate with the continual roar of aero engines. With the coming of winter there was peace again and only the cannonade of longshore gunners echoed across the dreary wastes of sand and saltings.

Landwards a line of trees marked the sea-wall, bent and twisted trees that had learnt the rude breath of the sea winds, winds that seldom slept. Beyond those trees the flat rich Fenlands stretched, dotted with glass-houses and prosperous farms, with never a hill and scarce a wood; a bitter land of toil and mist, devoid of noble mansions, devoid of beauty, devoted to the making of money and the sweating of labour. Ely lay beyond, a misty finger that brooded over the flat lands and reminded man there was still a God in heaven; Peterborough and Crowland, names that suggest the Viking raiders and the bitterns' boom.

As the tide fell, curlews began to flight in from the fields, calling one to the other in loud bell-like voices that carried some way across the saltings. They flew in formation, in V's and lines, seven or eight together, sometimes more.

Soon, on the velvet muds, pearly and moist, the tips of the samphire stalks appeared, sticking stiffly out of the cushions that were imprinted with the footmarks and claw marks of many wild creatures.

The winding runnels and creeks were everywhere; haphazard but efficient drains that had served their purpose for many thousands of years. Lying between two samphire stalks was the body of a black-backed gull, a handsome bird almost as big as a goose. Some shore gunner had shot it on the morning flight and it had journeyed out and in with the tides. It seemed perfect, no stain of blood or broken feather betrayed an injury, but nevertheless one single number four pellet had pierced the heart.

Two hooded crows, beating up the outmarsh, saw the body and circled round, cawing hoarsely, their wicked eyes fixed on the white spot below them. They pitched close beside the body, and after walking round with a waddling gait, took wing and flew away across the muds.

"Wheet, wheet," reeded the pipits, as they flicked above the sea lavender, pitching in the higher herbage out of the wind. They roosted out on this bleak place, and strangely enough it was warm down in the tangled roots of the lavender. There they could creep like mice, and only the tides disturbed them, or maybe a marsh harrier, hunting up the marshes.

As the light began to dim, toiling figures appeared, making their way across the marsh from the sea wall. Some had dogs at heel and carried guns. It was early yet for the duck flight, but the curlew were coming in now in bigger trips, and along the tide line a bunch of teal sped, whizzing like bullets just over the sand.

By now the gull's feather had cleared the outmarsh and was drifting down the main channel for the open sea. Little trips of wader flew past it, calling all together in thin voices, and two god-wits, probing the muds, watched it drift past them. As the tide fell, it seemed to gather speed, for in some of the guts and runnels the water was rushing in a turgid torrent, swirling over the mussel beds and talking about the base of a big weed-strewn buoy that now lay half on its side on the hard sand. Soon this buoy ceased to float and the water left its base. On one side there was a deep pool, hollowed by the action of the tides, and in this trap several dabs were flipping along the surface of the sand. They would have to remain there until the tide came back next morning.

Two redshanks rose shrieking from the bed of a gully and went away across the marsh, orange legs trailing, and their white wing bars showing vividly against the grey-green tones of the marsh.

They had been disturbed as they pattered over the smooth bed of a creek.

A man was coming along the top of the sea bank and as the redshanks flew away he came down from the sloping bank at a run and took a sheep track that wound out to the tide's edge. These sheep tracks were everywhere about the marshes, and served as useful short cuts for fowlers when the tide came in.

As he went along, pipits rose on either hand and flitted away, and a curlew rose from a little brackish pool that had been left by the last tide. "Curlee! Curlee!" it shrieked in a hoarse voice, and went out to the tide line where others of his kind were clustering in long line at the edge of the receding water.

"Foxy" Fordham knew these marshes like a book, for he had been born in the little village three miles away, where the ruined windmill stands. As a young man he had worked on the land and then he took to fowling. He had saved up enough money to buy a punt and after a while he found he could make more by selling his fowl than working for the farmer. "Foxy"—so called by men because he knew his craft so well, and also because he was the most skilful poacher in the district—was a man of middle height and broad shouldered. Ragged red bristles sprouted from his upper lip and his chin was seldom closely shaved. His eyes were never quite open and he always seemed to be peering out at life as it passed before the windows of his soul.

Not a bird, or a beast, could move without being quietly marked and noted by those keen eyes, and like an old fox that has learnt the craft of hunting, he had within him a sure knowledge of his livelihood. Not many cartridges were wasted when Foxy pulled the trigger, and if he missed his target he felt bad for hours afterwards.

On his head was a tattered cap, turned back to front, and he wore an old seaman's jersey, much darned by his thin little wife. On his legs were rubber thigh boots, the tops turned down so that he could walk more easily through the muds. And under his arm he carried a big rusty eight bore, the dearest thing he possessed —next to his dog.

Foxy treasured three things in life; his gun, his dog, and his gunning-punt. His wife and two pigs came next, and anything that contributed to his welfare was tolerated.

With a swinging gait he soon left the sea wall behind him and the herbage on the marsh grew shorter and the gullies wider. Now and again he would come to a deep drain and he crossed it with a practised leap, landing, well balanced, on the far side. The black and white cocker came after, ears flapping as he jumped.

After a while Foxy stopped and looked about him. His head was turned sideways, against the chirrup of the wind, and his eyes were fixed on the far line of water.

"Boomp!" a shot sounded away to the westward, down the marshes, and the screwed-up eyes swivelled round that way.

He noted a tiny figure, no bigger than a beetle, climb out of a gully and run across the salting to pick something up. "Some b—— shooting a curlew" thought Foxy. Then he turned his face to the sea again.

The light was failing now and all of a sudden it began to drain quickly, almost as he watched.

He looked about him and found a narrow "gull" scarce two feet across, but quite deep, and he lowered his rubber boots into this and sat down on the edge where the crab grass formed a wiry dry mattress.

His two great feet formed a dam in the trench, and very soon the water, draining from landwards, accumulated into quite a little lake, in which shrimps jerked about and a tiny crab sidled.

He took a well-seasoned pipe from his pocket and began to fill the bowl, pressing the rank shag down firmly with his broad, dirty fingers, with their split nails.

Close by, the dog sat watching every movement with a sulky expression set upon its mouth, because the upper lip had been caught up on a tooth. Now and again its brown eyes would scan the sky and follow the track of a passing gull. Line after line of gulls were now coming in off the fields, flying on set and lazy wings, gliding out to the sand banks where they would pass the night. Hardly had one group passed before another came in view, at first mere specks against the grey sky, and then clear and distinct.

Foxy moved his feet in the mud and released a torrent of water that swept down the gully bed and surprised a crab that was crawling along under the overhanging fringe of sea lavender. The smoke from his pipe was blown spinning away on the cold wind and the interior of the bowl glowed like a tiny forge.

Now a heron came, slow flagging and high, with the wind in his face. He was bound for the high sands and Frieston shore. All day he had been fishing the landward dykes and he was full fed and content. "Zank!" he cried when he saw the tiny figure far below, and flapped heavily onwards, lifting to each surge of wind.

Foxy now turned round and faced the sea, and one big thumb clicked back the hammers of his gun. The spaniel became more alert and kept on watching his master's face intently, for Foxy's eyes were on the greyness of the sky.

"Boomp!" ... "Boomp, boomp!" Shots began to sound, some near, some far, for the evening flight had begun.

Bang! Close at hand, and the dog jumped. Foxy turned a slow head and glanced idly along the marshes. Jim Barrit, the postman's son, got out of a creek and picked up a redshank. Foxy swore to himself and climbed out of his gully also. He walked away to the big main gully that feeds Long Drove End. A man could not be alone nowadays, there was always some pipit popper to spoil one's sport. . . . This main gully, known as the "main," was nearly thirty feet across and only wadable at low tide. Its slimy walls were seamed with glistening runnels that had eaten into the clay so that they were almost miniature gullies in themselves and in some places the mud was up to a man's thigh.

Foxy followed this down, until the gully divided into two channels, forming on one side, a bastion of clay.

This was a favourite spot, known only to Foxy, and he had shot many a duck and goose from this place.

He sat down again and repacked his pipe, and once more he cocked the hammers of the big gun.

Suddenly his eyes narrowed still more and he bent his head so that his eyes were on a level with the rim of the bank.

A hare was loping across the marsh, stopping ever and again to sniff the air with ears in a questioning V. It came nearer, and the heavy barrels crept up until the muzzle was resting among the sea lavender. Eighty yards, seventy . . . the hare stopped, looking directly in Foxy's direction, with its eyes dilated and nose working. The wind blew its fur so that it showed little blue tufts, but it could only see a distant redshank flickering over a dyke. Boomp! . . . The gun barrels seemed to jerk upwards and Foxy reeled back against the bank. The hare leapt skywards and fell back quivering, a blade of grass fixed firmly in its rat-like teeth.

From the far drain the cocker came tearing, ears flapping and with open mouth. It got a grip on the big body and went staggering back to Foxy.

Now the light was going fast, and the first mallard came over, high; so high that even the big eight-bore could not reach them, and Foxy's eyes watched them come and go, windborne, for the sea wall. Little stuttering quacks sounded on all sides as party after party came in, all too high with the wind behind them.

But Foxy had a comfortable feeling within, for he felt the warm bulge of the great hare inside his big bag, and knew his tramp had been worth while.

Westwards the sky was now still bright, but over the sea it was dark and darkening, even Foxy's eyes could not see the mallard if he looked that way; he had to turn so that he faced the last lingering light. Over the flats a line of stars began to dance and quiver as the ships and houses on the Boston side lit their lamps, and there came a great sense of loneliness and desolation, intensified by the querulous plainings of a green plover.

And then there came to Foxy a faint sound that was at first only intermittent. But the man seemed to rouse himself and his eyes almost opened wide.

"By Gor, if it ain't the geese!" he muttered, and climbed out of the Main.

The sound which was growing louder with the passing moments was like the far baying of hounds, the most wonderful music in the world. As it grew louder the various voices could be heard, deep-toned old ganders, and high, squeaking yelps intermingled, and yet there was still no sight of the geese. And then, very high against the last glim of the sunset he saw a long line of geese. They scattered as he watched them and seemed to tumble in the air, dropping like smuts from a chimney on to the high sands. As they lit on the banks they redoubled their clamour and then all was silent.

Only the rustle of the wind in the sea lavender and the "week, wee-week" of the green plover remained.

Foxy opened the door of his little cottage and stood for a moment blinking in the light of the room. His wife was beside the fire, sewing, and when she saw him she got up and went into the kitchen to prepare his supper—Foxy did not like to be kept waiting for his food.

The spaniel, wet and slimed with grey clay, stood patiently while the man rubbed him down with an old sack, and then went and curled up before the fire, watching the sparks burning a little chain on the soot of the chimney.

When Foxy had finished his supper and put his feet into some old slippers he lit his pipe and spoke.

"Th' geese cum in to-night, Mother, I 'eard 'em when I was up in the Main, a good pack on 'em too."

"Early, ain't they?"

"Ah, I reckon so."

"Where did 'ee get th' old 'are?"

"Up be the drain, cum runnin' across to me as I sat in the gull . . . a good un, ain't 'ee?"

Foxy took the stiff body off the table where grease and beer had stained the newspaper that served as a tablecloth and stroked the fine, handsome fur.

"That Jim Barrit were down on the outmarsh, the ——, 'ee's allus bangin' about there at pipits an' shank and such like."

The spaniel roused himself from the hearth and sniffed at the head of the hare as it hung down between Foxy's knees.

"'Ere, don't you dirty my floor, Fred, I cleaned un this after-noon."

Foxy took no notice, but went on stroking the fur. "Reckon I'll be after them old geese to-morrow mornin' on the flight, they'll very like be cummin' in over the Drain."

At that moment, the geese, sixteen tired birds, were asleep in the windy darkness on the high sands. The stars were hidden by scudding clouds and there was no moon.

Like the swallows, they had returned to their winter quarters, and the barrens and rocks of their summer home belonged to another world. For many hours their wings had borne them over countless miles, and they slept as deep as worn-out dogs. Nearly all had their bills tucked into their wings and not a bird was standing. All were resting their grey breasts on the sand and the tides swirled and sucked along the winding creeks unheeded.

Southwards a light grew and waned as the lightship on Boston Deep kept watch and ward, and beyond was the loom of another at the head of Lynn Deeps.

Occasionally a goose would shift his position, withdraw a sleepy head for a second, then tuck in its bill again with a weary gesture. Now and again a wader would flit by in the darkness, only its faint peeps betraying its swift passage, and from seawards came the low, windborne rustle of the flowing tide. Ever ceaseless, ever unwearied, the water was turning again for the land, and right out near Boston Deeps, the gull's feather was swaying this way and that as the tide took it.

Foxy Fordham was asleep, lying beside his thin little wife, his mouth open and softly snoring. He had taken off his trousers and boots, likewise his coat and shirt, but was sleeping in his underpants and vest. These he rarely took off unless he got a wetting in a creek.

The little room was in darkness and a cheap alarm clock ticked loudly on a chair by the bed.

And three miles away, out on the windy sands, buffeted by the sweet airs that came in unsullied from the North Sea, Manka slept, his pale pink bill, banded with black, tucked under the big feathers of his back. Foxy was dreaming of millions of geese that carpeted the sky and he was shooting at them with a pop-gun that fired corks. This enraged him so much he grumbled in his sleep, and stirred. "Fred, what be you at, carryin' on so, bide quiet can't ye?" Foxy grunted and turned over and a frightened mouse ran under the rickety washstand, for the mattress had squeaked.

A line of dancing fireflies over the Wash, jigging and flickering like remote stars, the louder rustle of the advancing tide, and the landward cocks calling up the dawn.

The big buoy was just beginning to float again and anxious dabs were flipping up to the edge of their sand crater, rejoicing in the new sweet water as it flowed into the basin.

Eastwards a greyness was creeping into the sky and along the roads workmen were cycling to another day's toil. Restless curlew, wide awake and calling, were flying down the tide, and ever and again a quick whistle of wings told that the mallard were coming out to sea.

All night long they had been in the drains and ponds inland, or grubbing in the stubbles. The hours of darkness were to them a cloak, that hid them from the eyes of enemies, ever ready to deprive them of the right to live.

And the gulls were waking, out on the high sands, preening and talking together and making ready for another day's work in the fields.

As the light grew, they began to rise in twos and threes and flew across the outmarsh, bound for the plough-lands where the kindly share clove apart the sheltering black loam and spread a breakfast for them. They would follow the plodding ploughman faithfully all day through, resting when he had his luncheon under a wind-blown hedge, to digest their morning's meal. To them, man was a friend and not an enemy, though London's "sportsmen," down for a day's fowling, sometimes shot at the beautiful white birds and left them to rot in a ditch.

And soon the curlew left the tide and, like the gulls, flew shore-wards, though with caution, for they feared the lurking guns.

All down the marshes of the East coast, a great exodus had begun, and as the light grew, millions of wildfowl left the sea and streamed towards the arable fields and farms.

Out on the sand-bank the geese, still weary, slept. Their wings were stiff with their long journey, and a man might have walked on them as they slumbered, for even their sentries slept. It was as if a weary army camped there on the sand, rank on rank of grey-uniformed birds, oblivious of the growing dawn.

But soon the sea grew bright in the dawn light, gleaming like a sheet of silver to the east, and the trees along the sea wall became distinct and black. One by one the geese awoke. Some stretched a broad, grey-mantled wing over outstretched pink paddle, others began to feel among their soft breast feathers and pass low, guttural remarks in conversational tones.

Manka awoke too, and stretched his neck like a farmyard goose, and the feathers on his head stood up for a moment. Then he shook himself all over, as a dog shakes water from his coat, and he took several paces to the edge of the gaggle. His fine head, with a neck the colour of old snow, was erect and creased with furrows, and his pale eyes—unlike those of his brethren, which were brown—scanned the wastes of sand around him.

He could see the buoy floating above the sand, erect also, and beginning to bob gently to the feel of the tide. He saw the yellow water moving steadily up the big creek on the left of the sandbank, bearing its clots of scummy foam. And he felt the dawn wind among his feathers and he shook himself again.

On all sides crowded the motionless army of geese, some still deep in sleep with bills hidden in their backs, though one or two, on the outskirts of the gaggle, were walking down to the edge of the banks.

Manka went too, not with the ungainly waddle of the domestic goose, but with proud, upright carriage, dignity and grace. He went along the sand, between the sleeping geese, and entered the shallow water, dibbling with his bill and rubbing the back of his head on his mantle. His neck was as sinuous as a snake's body, and he could turn his head almost right round.

He had a bath in the shallow water, and felt the ripple of the tide going over his broad paddles. Then he stalked out again and rejoined the army.

All were awake now, and some were honking, a loud, resonant sound, that carried a long way over the flats, "Ank! . . . Ank! . . . Anka!"

It was still very dark in the little bedroom, the alarm clock was ticking loudly in the quiet. Foxy lay on his back snoring, and beside him was the draggled black bun of his wife's hair, looking like a cat on the grubby pillow.

The clock went off into a sudden scream that died and slowed, and ceased. After this hysterical outburst it ticked quietly on and the spaniel in the basket roused himself and sat up.

Foxy stirred and grunted, and his wife turned over and muttered. "Urgh . . . aah!" groaned Foxy and opened his eyes. He climbed out of bed and stretched.

"What time will you be back, Fred?" said a sleepy voice from the bed.

"Oh, dunno, nineish or thereabouts, reckon I might get one o' them old geese."

He lit a candle and put on his trousers and boots, and the spaniel hopped out of its basket and came across to him. He went into the kitchen and cut himself a crust of bread, giving some to the attendant spaniel, and then he unhooked the gun from over the door, where he always kept it. From an orange box on a side-table he took a handful of cartridges and stuffed them into his pocket. Then he left his sleeping wife and opened the door.

The clouds had blown away, the stars were showing, and the keen cold of dawn took him by the throat and made him cough. When Foxy reached the sea road, with its line of twisted oaks that formed an avenue for a quarter of a mile before it took a right-angled turn for the Bank, the light was growing bright in the East and the teams were being taken to the plough lands.

Passing workmen, when they saw the familiar figure stumping up the puddled road, hailed him. "'Lo, Foxy, arter them old ducks?" . . . "Morn', Foxy, don't shoot 'em all!" . . . some just said "'Ullo, Foxy," and passed on, their glimmering bicycle lamps wavering on the road in front.

As soon as the man topped the sea wall, a gust of cold wind hit him a buffet in the face. It was blowing hard off the sea, though back on the land he had not noticed it.

Across the Wash the lights of Boston were paling, like the stars, and wood pigeons, that had been roosting in the trees along the sea bank, clattered away into the duskiness. These birds roosted every night in the sea wall oaks, and strangely enough, rusty leaves clung to their branches most of the winter, even though the trees had to stand the buffets of winter gales.

Below the sea wall, on the landward side, was a long creek that was now shining brightly in the dawn light, and screaming redshanks rose from its muddy margin, and flickered away.

He turned left by the shepherd's cottage, and walked along the sea wall, following the telegraph wires. Every pole was thrumming in the wind, singing a wild song all its own, a lonely lullaby that rarely was stilled. Even on the calmest summer's evening, if you put your ear to the wood, you could hear a gentle murmur, as when one listens to a shell.

Trip after trip of curlew were coming off the outmarsh as Foxy went along the wall, and some passed within gunshot. The man did not fire at them, however, for ducks and geese commanded a better market.

He turned his eyes constantly towards the land, for incoming mallard were still flighting out to the flats.

The spaniel ran along the foot of the bank, sniffing about amongst the sea lavender, and splashing through the little flashes. Soon he saw a figure approaching along the crest of the bank, and the shepherd stopped when he saw Foxy, to pass the time of day. "Ole geese come in last night, Foxy." The shepherd, Billy Minns, leant on his crook and spat.

He was a short, wiry man with a thin face, and as hard as nails. He pastured nearly a thousand sheep on the marshes for his master, and was a good shepherd.

"Ah, I 'eered 'em, Billy, nice gang too . . . 'ark!"

From the high sands there came a gabbling of voices, deep croaks and high squeaks.

The geese were all awake now, and walking about in groups,

Manka flying over the Sassen Marshes

all had been down to the water and they were strolling this way and that, waiting as if for some pre-arranged signal.

"Reckon I'll be gettin' down the ole creek, Billy."

"Ah . . . well, morn' Foxy!"

It was now so clear that Foxy could almost see the geese as they rested on the sandbanks. He was late . . . folk would stop and talk . . . and he hurried across the marsh, springing the deeper gullies with many grunts.

He reached the main drain and his favourite hiding-place, and quickly got under cover, for the geese would be in any moment. He could see the buoy out in the channel, and very faintly, to southward, the Air Force targets, rising like the bones of some long-forgotten wreck above the sands.

Anka! Anka! Ank! Ank! Ankquee! Quee Quee! Much conversation out on the sands!

The white goose, standing on the outskirts of the flock began to run into the wind. The great moment had come, their bellies were empty after their long journey and they must feed.

It was a wonderful sight as the whole army took the air. Four or five quick steps along the sand and they felt the air under their wings, and there was a roar and a rush that sent Foxy flat into the bottom of the dyke. Though he had been a fowler for thirty years and more and had shot hundreds of geese, that sound never failed to quicken his pulses.

As the geese got on the wing they broke into a perfect tornado of gabbling that could have been heard for over a mile. From their hanging paddles the stars of water dropped, and the broad, grey wings took firm hold on the solid air and made it tremble. For a few yards they beat into the wind, then wheeled, and Foxy, crouching in the ditch, caught his breath.

He watched the wheeling skein come round into the wind, he saw them take formation as a flight of aeroplanes on manœuvres will fall into place, and he saw they would pass a long gun-shot off.

They came, low at first, over the marsh, then rising as they sensed the land. By the time they passed Foxy, at well over a hundred yards, they were nearly two hundred feet high, and climbing all the time.

Third in line was Manka, the early morning sun shining full upon him so that he seemed as white as a gull.

Foxy, hunched in his gully, watched them go, his heart beats slowing, and the big eight-bore returned to the crook of his arm.

And he made a vow that whatever happened, he would shoot Manka. It was to become his one ambition, it was a challenge to his powers and to the knowledge of his craft. Manka should be his, some time, somewhere. He would wait, he would watch, and in the end he would get him.

Just as some men set their minds on a high ideal, and work for that day and night, dream about it and scheme about it, so Foxy resolved to have Manka's skin.

Two late mallard passed over unheeded, Foxy's eyes were fixed on the dwindling arrowhead of geese, and he heard the clamour dying as they sped towards the land.

Shardwaner's farm was one of the largest in East Anglia. Generations of Shardwaners had been at Maplode St. Marks and they were almost kings in their own country.

When mechanical labour replaced the old-fashioned methods, the Shardwaners were the first to look ahead and realize what was to come. They purchased all the latest machines; binders, reapers, and tractors, and prided themselves in being ahead of their neighbours in all things. Therefore they prospered and grew rich. They enlarged the old farmhouse and built many greenhouses, for tomato growing was becoming a profitable industry. From the rich, dark soil they produced some of the finest potatoes in Britain and the pay roll grew year by year until it was nearly two hundred pounds a week.

They ran three cars—one a Rolls—had they been in a hunting country they would have aspired to being "County."

The two sons went to one of the more famous public schools and the daughter was "finished" in Paris.

For miles around Maplode one would see carts inscribed with the illustrious name of Shardwaner, creaking along the level roads, laden with farm produce for the big London markets.

As is often the case in more isolated communities, the family ramified and spread to the country around. They built and bought other farms and, as it was in the blood, and they could reap the benefit of experience, they likewise prospered.

Old Mr. Dick Shardwaner was the patriarch of the tribe; he it was that built the village hall in Maplode and gave a thousand pounds to the local hospital. People would say of him, with a shake of the head, "Ah . . . th' old gentleman must be worth a tidy bit, wouldn't mind 'arf what 'ees got, and then 'ee'd never notice it."

Many a pheasant did Foxy have off the Shardwaners' land, and many a partridge, too, for the land was crawling with game. In the autumn, when the harvest was in, there was a big harvest home in the vast barn behind Mellons Platt, the Shardwaners' house, and everyone had as much beer as they liked. Later, when the sere leaves had mellowed and dropped from the lime avenue, there would be pheasant shoots, and the farmers for miles around would come. Then the sound of the shots disturbed the waders on the marshes and terrified pheasants came creeping over the sea wall for the shelter of the gullies.

Foxy, who always knew beforehand, partly by instinct, that a shoot was going to take place, would be there, waiting for them; one evening he shot fourteen pheasants, all on the salt marshes.

But he did not always wait for them to come on the outmarsh, he stalked them behind the wall in the early morning, just when they were "cocking" as they smelt the dawn, and many a bird did he have in this way; partridges too, fell to his gun.

He rarely ate game, but took them in to a friend of his, a "fence," who paid him well for his pains.

And it says something for his cunning that in thirty years poaching he had never been caught. Twice old Mr. Shardwaner had chased him—when he was a younger man—but Foxy got away; once by lying in a gully up to his neck in water, and once by swimming. He lost his gun that time, and had to retrieve it next day.

On the western boundary of the Shardwaners' farm there was a field over a hundred acres in extent, bounded on one side by six pollarded elms that leant with their bristly tops pointing to the East.

This field was visible from the Boston road and was a favourite winter resort for the pink-footed geese.

Old Mr. Shardwaner only shot them twice during the winter, once at the end of November and again just after Christmas.

Many people went up and down on the highway and never noticed the grey blobs on the plough, or if they did, thought they were domestic geese.

But when the long lines of geese came in from the sea, waving from end to end like a wagging scarf, strangers to the district would stop their cars to watch them, wondering maybe what manner of strange fowl they were.

For the next few weeks after the geese arrived they used this field, known as Leader's Drove, with great regularity, flighting in from the sea, morning after morning, in V's and arrowheads.

They saw at first the sand, skimming beneath their pink paddles as they began to climb. Then the little marsh plants clustering the muds, then the winding creeks and grey-green marsh herbage and the sea-bank, topped with the telephone wires. By that time they would be a hundred yards or more high, and the country unfolded beneath them until they could see the tall church spires of Holbeach and Long Sutton, and the clustering red roofs of King's Lynn. Behind them the basin of the Wash, gleaming like a great dish, and at last, below, the clustering trees about Mellons Platt, the glass-houses, and pond at the end of the paddock, appearing no larger than a threepenny bit.

Behind Mellons Platt the white gulls clustering about the plough-man, and all about, like spiders' webs, the network of dykes and levels, willow girt and bright.

Then, breaking formation they would wheel, high in the sky trumpeting wild music one to the other so that even the labourers in the fields would raise their wee, pale faces skywards. Poor little ants of men! Chained to the ground, beetle-wise, doomed to toil among the dust from the cradle to the grave!

Scattering, now, they would dive headlong towards the earth, sideslipping down in quick twists, on to the centre of Leader's Drove.

Towards noon, when the men ceased work in the fields and had a snack under a hedge, the geese would sit about on the furrows, digesting the potatoes, and preening, and would frequently go back to the sea for a wash and brush up. It was on these daylight flights that men marked Manka, shining as white as a homing pigeon against the grey sky, leading the big skeins over the sea wall.

They would rest on their hoes and watch the geese pass. . . . "There's t'old white 'un agin, Tom, I seed him these last few mornins'."

"I bet ole Foxy 'ud give summat for a chance at 'im. . . ."

"Ah! . . ."

When the sun slanted behind the pollarded elm trees, and the long roads were dotted with weary men returning to their homes, the geese would rise from Leader's Drove in a clamouring pack, circling the fields and farms before going out to sea. Then, as the light dimmed and the sun sank they went out to where the sounding buoys rolled in the heaving swells and the greater black gulls croaked their heavy, flapping way, across the misty solitudes. A world of mist and rustlings, of wind and spray, of sea voices and wind voices, a refuge from mankind.

You may be sure Foxy marked Manka, many a day, as the white

goose stalked, vividly, upon the dark plough or flew with the rest of the skein over the outmarsh on the evening flight. And he realized that soon the geese would be "shot up" on Leader's Drove, and might go away for the rest of the winter, and his chance would be gone. So he schemed and plotted to gain his ends . . . somehow, somewhere . . . in his own time. . . .

The lime-tree avenue to Mellons Platt sent its leaves spinning, disclosing unexpected beauty in their delicate twig traceries.

Old Mr. Shardwaner and his farmer friends tramped the stubbles, and the report of their guns made the labourers pause in their work. Pop . . . pop . . . pop . . . through the soft, grey afternoons. The redwings and fieldfares came, and spread about the fields, and the first woodcocks, flying the marshes like tired moths, many falling to the guns of lurking fowlers as they waited for duck up at Horseshoe Gull.

Along the wide plains the twitch fires sent long ribbons of sweet blue smoke, and mallard flew restlessly about the dykes. The November moon waxed to the full, magnified to twice its size by the evening mists, the colour of a Dutch cheese.

Then, in those days, the geese no longer came to Leader's Drove in the day time. They slept out on the sands and came in after the moon was up, so that men should not see them. But they came with just as much noise, and they passed over Mellons Platt like shouting demons, clustering shadows against a world of stars. Manka usually lay second or third in the skein, though he sometimes led them.

The fields and marshes appeared so different in the moonlight, and the wide lands, with scarce a hedge between, greenish plains of vast extent. Then the shadows of the geese were ghostly and black as they stalked about the furrows or on the stubble lands, and they had to keep a weather eye open for foxes, and creeping gunners about the sea wall.

One moonlight night towards the end of November, Foxy formed a plan. He learnt by rumour—and intuition—that the

Shardwaners were going to shoot the geese on Leader's Drove at the end of the week, and if Manka was to be shot it would have to be before that day, as in all probability, the geese would go away to another part of the coast.

On the Tuesday evening of that week he left his house just after eight o'clock and took the path along the sea bank. When he reached Horseshoe Gull he struck across the fields, crossing the dyke by the little plank bridge.

He had left his dog at home, for on such forays he preferred to work entirely alone.

After crossing two fields he came to a stretch of plough, and this he followed for half a mile.

One tiny orange window watched him for a long while, from the shepherd's cottage, but at last a rise in the ground hid it from view, and he felt suddenly alone.

Restless peewits, camping on the plough, heard and saw the dark figure coming along the headland, and rose, wavering and calling . . . Pew . . . weeet! . . . Pee weeet! "Damn them birds!" thought Foxy. He stopped.

Behind him there was a faint reddish glow over the sea bank; soon the moon would be up and the geese would be in, also the figure of a man would be visible from some distance. Foxy did not want to be seen.

There seemed not a soul about on Leader's Drove when Foxy reached the edge of the plough. Beyond the far hedge, a motor-car, heading Boston way, sent a pencil of light moving across the furrows but not a bird whistled or a dog barked.

Foxy went along by the side of the dyke until he had reached a point half-way across the field.

A deep dyke ran the whole length of Leader's Drove on the eastern side, crossed at one end by a plank. This led to another big arable field, and beyond that was the sea wall.

The man found a hollow in the side of the bank and sat down, constantly turning his head this way and that like a guilty dog.

From far to seawards came the bumping, throaty boom of a ship's siren, going down on the tide, and occasionally a reedy piping betrayed a passing wader as it flitted across the big field. Golden plover were out on Leader's Drove, they roosted there, and after a while Foxy began to hear their flute-like pipes as they flighted about. Goldens are restless little folk, like all the plovers, and never seemed to roost for long.

From the bailiff's farm a dog started to bark and this sound, so associated with humankind, made Foxy feel uneasy, and he turned his face in that direction.

After a while the sound ceased and the glow over the rim of the sea wall intensified until the edge of the moon rose solemnly, red and large, magnified by the sea mists.

All around now those great, flat fields were sleeping; ancient lands that somehow breathed adventure and romance.

From every lonely farmhouse shone a light, as families clustered round the fire in the stuffy rooms. How blind man is, what magic here under the rising moon!

Before very long a mallard began to quack, quite close by somewhere in the dyke. Quar! Quar! Quar! Quar! Quar! Foxy lay still. Soon the sea began to glitter like metal under the moon's path, and shadows were thrown from every post and reed.

It was a mild night, and Foxy found his leather waistcoat irksome. But he did not remove it for fear of being obliged to take rapid and prudent flight.

The mallard in the dyke suddenly rose and flew away; Foxy could hear the passage of its wings and little stuttering quacks as it went away for the sea wall.

At night these fields were alive with ducks of all descriptions; mallard, wigeon, pochard and teal.

Now and again a car would pass along the road and he could hear the drone of its engine and then—a man, riding a motor-bike and singing at the top of his voice. The machine droned like a bee and above it he could hear the notes of the song.

How quiet it was here! . . . Slowly the sound died away, the man's voice persisting above the engine of his mount, until both blended and died. And still the geese did not come. Foxy lit a pipe. He did not usually smoke when on his poaching forays, but now boredom had to be relieved, and he was dying for a "spit and draw."

In the dyke the reeds stood, withered and slender, and something came swimming down the drain, shaking the moon's reflection.

It was an otter, eel hunting. It passed close to Foxy, moving without a sound, with little kicks of its rudder, looking like a huge water-rat. The ripples of its wake lapped quietly among the reeds and calmed.

Foxy thought of the village ale-houses, the Dog and Gun at Drovefleet, the Black Swan at Gunders End . . . crowded tap-rooms, tobacco smoke and the hum of man's talk. It was better here.

A shadow passed across the moon, a shadow like some dark angel, winging a way over the flat lands. "Krank!" one harsh cry and a heron passed over Leader's Drove on his way to Mudhorse Hole, a wide creek that ran into the sea beyond the bailiff's house. There was no cloud or wreath of mist; above, an ocean of stars, seawards the calm moon, rising and surveying all.

On the bank of the dyke the shadow of Foxy was inky and hardly moved, it was part of the dyke, of the bank, of Leader's Drove.

Now like a rush of spirits, some golden plover came, flying in a great crowd and piping shrilly, sad little pipes that came down out of the spangled dome above like drops of silver rain. A bird came over the sea bank and flew, noisily, over the furrows. It was a pheasant that had been down on the outmarsh for salt. Foxy's pipe went out, and he refolded the sack that served him as a seat.

Damn the geese, when would they come? Eleven o'clock struck from Maplode St. Mark's church, and a curlew flew over, bound for the saltings.

Foxy lit another pipe and stood up and stretched. Faint clouds were massing over the sea, woolly white filmlets that came gently across the sky and veiled, momentarily, the moon.

And then there came from seawards the faint honking of a single goose. It called at intervals, each time drawing nearer, and Foxy got down again into his ditch. Though he did not see it, it passed, from the sound, over Leader's Drove, circling once or twice and then went away to sea again, its voice dying into the distance. The far bump of a punt gun sounded from the Boston side and all again was still.

The otter came back up the dyke, swimming this time on the far side, but it must have winded Foxy, for it dived before it came abreast of the hiding man.

And then Foxy heard the geese leave the sea.

Though they had been out on the sand bars over a mile away, he heard them take the air. From the sound they had split up into several parties, some going down the coast towards King's Lynn, and the others circling back and heading for Leader's Drove.

Very soon he heard them over Mellons Platt, then towards Maplode, then coming straight for him, baying like hounds in the moonlight.

They circled wide—Foxy still could not see them—and for some reason went away to the north, and all again was silent. Foxy cursed and got up again, walking down the side of the dyke. Then he stopped. A figure was coming along the sea wall. . . . He was aware of this person before he could see him, or even hear him. Some sixth sense told him someone was approaching, and he got down into the reeds that grew along the edge of the dyke. Soon he heard voices, low conversational voices, and knew that there was more than one person. They were coming straight for the plank bridge, and Foxy debated what he was to do.

Crouching down in the reeds he was quite invisible, and he decided the best policy would be to wait until they had passed. Soon he saw their reflections in the water and saw there were three men, with guns, and followed by a dog. They came along the edge of the dyke, and would pass directly above Foxy. So he pressed himself down among the reeds and lay without a rustle.

"Jim, you go along beyond the foot bridge, I'm getting down here in the dyke. . . . All right. . . ." A dark figure came rustling through the reeds towards Foxy, and it seemed as if he must be found, but still he lay, though his heart was bumping in his ears. He recognized the voice and build of young Mr. Shardwaner, young Mr. Jeremy. Jeremy could run, and Foxy knew it and was miserable.

But before he came within twenty yards of the hiding man, he climbed on the top of the bank again and walked along the side of the dyke, within a few feet of Foxy, and got down in a hollow about forty yards below. The dog (a spaniel) came rustling through the reeds to where Foxy was crouching and stopped when it saw him, with dilated eyes. Then it came and sniffed him gingerly, and Foxy patted its head.

"Here . . . Donna! . . . come here." The man whistled, and the spaniel trotted away in the moonlight.

Foxy was in a ticklish position and did not quite know what to do. It annoyed him that he should have so misjudged the night. Had he been here yesterday all would have been well, he had seen the geese come in to Leader's Drove as soon as the moon rose, for he had been on the sea wall, and ten to one the white goose was with them. That he should just have happened on this night, of all nights, annoyed him very much.

But young Mr. Jeremy was not a good fowler, because he was not patient, and after waiting for half an hour, and no sign of the geese, Foxy heard him whistling the dog and going off down the dyke to join his companions.

Discretion being the better part of valour, Foxy retired gracefully, under the cover of the bank, to the plank bridge, and crossed the next field to the sea bank. Once he thought a man shouted after him, but he stayed not upon the order of his going.

A little after two in the morning he heard the geese coming back from the direction of Lynn, and they settled on Leader's Drove. Not a shot went off. Young Jeremy and his friends, tired of waiting, had gone home, and the geese fed in peace, until the first hint of dawn bade them fly for the open sea.

On the Friday evening the Shardwaners again planned an ambush at Leader's Drove.

The geese had used the field more or less continuously since the first week of November, and it must have been pure bad luck that they had drawn a blank on the Tuesday evening.

On the Wednesday and Thursday nights the geese came in as soon as the moon was up, but as it was waning they came in later every night.

Seven guns assembled in the stone-flagged parlour and the gravel sweep in front of Mellons Platt seemed full of cars. At half-past nine, young Jeremy went out and had a look at the night, and found it overcast, with a strong breeze off the sea. Visibility was bad for shooting, but they decided to go, and after many bottles of beer had been disposed of, they set out for Leader's Drove. Foxy, strolling along the sea road, saw the guns setting out, and then he went back to the Drum and Monkey for a drink.

"Well, Foxy, got that old white goose yet?" "Reckon 'e'll beat you, Foxy." "Stick to 'un Foxy, you'll get 'im next year." "Bet you a quid you don't shoot 'im this winter, Foxy!"

The last speaker, a bricklayer from Long Drove Dyke, took a pull at his beer and set the glass, streaked with froth, on top of the bar.

Foxy vouchsafed no reply, but rapped on the counter for a pint o' mild. "Shardwaners are shooting Leader's Drove agin to-night. Look well if the young —— shoots 'im, Foxy, 'ee ain't a bad shot! . . . 'Ark!"

Above the murmur of the taproom there came the distant pop of guns, and Foxy and the bricklayer went to the door and stood in the road.

The wind was creaking in the old windmill and whistling in the thorns of the roadside hedges, and a few faint stars were showing. Behind the inn there was a vague luminosity, for the moon was climbing, veiled in scudding clouds, and it seemed a good night for shooting. Pop, pop, two more shots, and to the listening men came the faint clamour of the wild geese as they circled Mellons Platt.

"'Avin' some shots, any road," said the bricklayer, and went back into the bar. Foxy stood along in the roadway, and then walked away down the lane towards the sea wall.

Manka and his brethren walked into the wind and took the air. They were hungry and the moon was up, shining dimly on the wet sands as the clouds came and went.

Wheeling, they passed over the buoy, and headed for the land and Leader's Drove. The sea bank was passed, and the half circle of Horseshoe Gull, and they passed, with bands playing, over the clustering trees of Mellons Platt.

They came in low for Leader's Drove, for they suspected nothing, four weeks they had fed and never a gun was fired at them.

Leader's Drove looked inviting, spread out below them, and they thought of the feed awaiting them, caution went to the winds. They saw the haystack in the corner and the long potato camps, the dyke, brimming with tide, and the plank bridge, and they dropped their paddles for the landing.

Then from the dark crease of the dyke, hell broke loose, stabs of red flame darting upwards, the dry thunderclap of shots. The big, grey goose ahead of Manka gave a cry, a cackle cut short and ending in a squark, and he slumped down under Manka's tail. Two pellets of BB shot sang through Manka's left wing, cutting one of his strong flight-feathers clean away, and he tipped up his head and took hold of the air, thrusting it from him with rapid wing beats so that he towered towards the stars.

The rest of the flock had scattered on the instant and were heading all ways, some going over Mellons Platt, others to sea and the sea wall, yet several more breaking back towards the Boston road. They came together again, calling now once more—during and just after the firing they had been silent—and now they took stations again, and held out for the sandbanks.

Five of their number were left behind on the dark earth, ten wings would never beat the air again.

One young bird, hatched on the Esker bluffs, was scuttling like a frightened hare over the field, and somewhere behind a panting spaniel was nose down on its trail. He never gained the dyke, for the spaniel pinned him within thirty yards of it and there was a battle of wings, and feathers flew until a man came across the furrows and knocked the goose on the head.

Within an hour the other section of Manka's army, which had been roosting farther along the coast, came over to Leader's Drove and found it strangely quiet.

They passed, gaggling for a reply, over the dyke, and again the guns spoke, three geese falling to rise no more.

Manka, at the peak of the arrowhead, went far down the coast, and they came down on Richards' farm, on the Long Sutton side. There they fed unmolested until dawn, when they went back to sea, and safety.

When Manka preened his wing on the sandbank he felt one stump of a feather, and he worried at it with his banded bill. A tiny bit of fluff fell out of his wing and was caught up by the wind. It blew across the flat sand, rolling over and over, until it reached the flowing tide and was carried away.

Wells Beach

Eastwards the sky was lightening and the lamps in the farmhouse went out.

They would leave Leader's Drove, for death was there, lurking in every shadow.

The November moon waned and the nights grew dark again. More geese came in during the first week in December and "used" many of the fields around Mellons Platt, some falling to the gunners hidden in the outmarsh dykes, and no less than seventeen to the guns of Shardwaner and his friends, for the first goose shoot had been counted a failure.

Also the mild weather still held, and not an ice crystal was to be seen, even in the early mornings, on the puddles of the marsh road.

Shepherd Billy never remembered so mild a time and the ancients wagged their heads, foretelling dire cold before the winter was over.

The open weather suited the geese, they could feed on the potato fields and fare was plentiful.

Foxy Fordham tramped the marshes many mornings, but though he saw the long, wavering lines of geese coming in from the sand bars, he searched in vain for the far flicker of a white wing. Manka and forty of his brethren had moved down the coast to a different land. No longer were there flat fields and glass houses, straight dykes and no trees. It was a land of sand dunes and marram grass, wide sandy flats on which the North Sea thundered, and small marshes where cattle grazed, little dykes, and "flashes" full of teal and mallard. Landwards were woods and great estates, well keepered and preserved, fat farm lands with rich stubbles, heathery wastes and scattered firs.

They roosted out on the sand bars beyond Wells, and as the skein leader knew every inch of the country as intimately as a six-year-old swallow knows his own barn, he led his clamouring army over Holkham Gap, high above the little pop-guns of fine-weather fowlers. He was aware, too, of the danger of the lying-pits men made out on the sands, and every little stump of drift wood was investigated first, from a height of a hundred yards and more, before he took his army down.

Men saw Manka, shining white like a pigeon against the grey sky, and he was the talk of Wells.

Chapter Four
THE FENS

Those days were spent grazing on the short, sweet grass and flights over the fir woods to the high stubbles inland. At evening they would come in, long clamouring lines that wove and interwove, crossing the blue woodlands and great houses where smoke rose straight against bare trees, to the wide sandbanks beyond Holkham Gap.

ON that North Norfolk coast, with its shifting sand-hills and lonely marshy fields, intersected by long, rushy dykes, the geese were less disturbed.

Most of the land was privately owned; on the Holkham estate the geese fed in safety for nobody was allowed to come after them. And with the silencing of guns the geese became more trusting, feeding close beside the railway, heedless of passing trains. It would be hard to imagine a more striking contrast between this rich, green country, with its great estates and dense woods swarming with game, and the half-made world of ice and glacier across the sea.

Like all wild birds, geese have an uncanny sense of danger and know full well when they can feed in peace.

Day succeeded day, mild and open, thrushes singing in the short twilight, well-fed, sleek cattle cropping the grass of the inland meadows with the peaceful ease of summertime. Those days were spent grazing on the short, sweet grass and flights out over the fir woods to the high stubbles inland. At evening the long clamouring lines would come in, weaving and interweaving over the blue woodlands and the great houses where smoke rose straight against bare purple trees, heading for the wide sandbanks beyond Holkham Gap.

Happy gatherings in the pastures where wagtails "chissicked" and white gulls kept good company, days of rest, of ease, of plenty.

All manner of birds thronged these low meadows; trim, gold-spangled plovers, the larger crested green lapwings, redshanks by the score, every ditch and drain held snipe and teal. At nights, when the geese had gone out to sea and a sliver of a moon came over the black belt of firs, the mallard came whistling in from the banks to feed all night long in these marshy meadows. Manka was not the only big white bird that fed upon the fields. One day a long-legged fellow with a spoon-shaped bill appeared. He had come overnight from the Zuider Zee. It was a spoonbill, once a common enough bird in that part of the country; he had been banished by the march of time, the draining of the fens, and all the "improvements" of our modern world. He was as shy, or shyer, than the geese. He fed up the little drains, walking sedately and scooping his long spoon from side to side, dredging out all the tasty little morsels. Often he hopped out to see if the coast was clear and never remained for long below the level of the bank.

And then came the time when the numbers of geese using the marshes was doubled and trebled. Every day more geese came in and not all of them were pink-feet. There were several skeins of white-fronted geese, held by some to be handsomest of all the wild geese, with their bright orange legs and white foreheads.

O' nights now they had to run the gauntlet of the Wells gunners who lined the bank behind the belt of firs. Most of the shots were taken when the geese were far out of range, for it was only in windy weather they flew low. But the firing worried them and spent shot rattled on their broad vanes. It was trying to the nerves. They moved quarters farther up the coast, haunting the marshes by Brancaster and Cley, where tall grey towers stood sentinel over the sea, and in the harbours and creeks many dinghies rode at anchor with bare poles. Their red sails would run up again in the August blue, when the heat mists quivered over the creeks and a dazzle shook the air beyond the sand dunes.

There were many little flashes on the surface of the marsh and the feeding was good. But there was not the security and peace of the Holkham marshes, and after lingering awhile, they moved on northwards, past Hunstanton and King's Lynn, to the old familiar ground about the Wash.

The change of food was good after grass, especially the salty grass of the marshes, and Manka waxed fat on the young wheat and old potatoes. There were guns lining the sea wall every morning, but the Wash is such a vast expanse, it would take a battalion of soldiers to cover every yard of the bank. Though a shot or two was fired when they went in to the fields of a morning, they frequently passed out unmolested.

Foxy soon knew the geese were back, and he nearly bit his pipe-stem in two one morning when he glimpsed the white wings of Manka beating against the dark clouds of departing night.

"Ole white goose be back," said Billy the shepherd as he met Foxy by his cottage.

Foxy leant the gun against the fence and puffed at his pipe. His eyes were never still, they roved the marsh, the far, flat fields, the sea wall, marking the flight of every gull and wader.

"Ah, I seed 'im, Billy, a beauty 'e is. I'll 'ave 'im in me own time, you see."

Foxy was not usually so communicative, but Billy was rather a friend of his, because he never "spilt the beans" when he saw Foxy poaching on the Shardwaners' land.

"Look well if one of those London shooters popped 'im off, Foxy."

Foxy spat an incredible distance, and leant his elbows on top of the tarred rail. He was watching the yellow water coming up under the trestle bridge, the slow spinning cakes of froth pushed along by the flowing tide.

"Ah! they can't shoot, most on 'em couldn't 'it your cottage yonder!"

"Not all on 'em, Foxy, I saw one down two wi' one shot

last month along the bank, spankin' buds they was too, fat as butter."

"I seed 'im," said Foxy, "I seed 'im. You could 'a knocked 'em down wi' your crook in that mist."

The morning had come and the sun shone redly among the upper whippy twigs of the poplars along the sea wall.

The shepherd looked at the sky.

"Seems to me we're going to 'ave some 'ard weather fairly soon, my water-butt were froze this mornin'."

High in the sunlight golden plover were passing over, piping one to another. Peet! then a pause, then Peet! It was a plaintive little pipe, full of sorrow and wildness.

Foxy did not reply. He was watching a heron labouring out over the bank on its way to fish for eels in Horseshoe Gull. All the geese had long gone inland, only curlew and gulls specked the sky at intervals.

There was that clean-washed look about the sky and the marshes, a clarity of atmosphere that was almost a glaze. And the morning smelt good, too, strong with the tang of the sea. But Foxy did not see the beauty of the morning, the sun on the sea wall trees, or the long, straight ribs of glistening plough. He only saw a snow-white goose flying high against a dark cloud, a white tip to an arrow that pointed to the land.

In his own time, somehow, somewhere, Manka should be his. Foxy was a man in whom the hunting instinct was a vice. As some men crave for drink or women, Foxy craved to kill. But he killed only those animals and birds that could be used for the pot. True, if he saw a rare bird (and rare species were sometimes seen on those bleak marshes) he would shoot it in the hope of making money out of it. But he did not slaughter the gulls and fairy-like waders, as did the visiting gunners who came in noisy sports cars, and left the pathetic little corpses to bob away on the tide.

Foxy was a man to whom pity was unknown, he was as merciless as a stoat.

From beyond Mellons Platt came the baying of geese, and Foxy's head slewed sideways. A long string of black beads waved in the sunlight and slanted down towards Leader's Drove. Foxy's mouth opened slightly to disclose the yellow rabbit-tooth.

Over the field the geese wheeled and then side-slipped, the wind thrumming in their vanes. Manka's wings fanned forward three times and folded themselves over his back, the stability of the air became the rock stability of the ground. He looked about him and cocked one eye skywards at other geese which, cackling loudly, were landing all around him.

The gaggle stood for some moments with poker-like necks, scanning the surrounding fields. Every clod, every bush, came under that scrutiny from hundreds of pairs of sharp little brown eyes. Then Manka stretched forth his neck, just like the old gander in the Shardwaners' yard and shook himself.

He lifted one pink paddle over one white wing and scratched the side of his bill. Then he waggled his tail like a duck, fanning it and shaking it and rolling his head on his soft broad back. Every now and then he ceased his toilet to look about him. Other geese were preening, some were beginning to take nervous plucks at the springing blades of wheat. The sun shone warm and the gin-clear air was full of sunlight and gull voices. Away in the distance was the restless hiss of the sea and the bleating of sheep pastured on the marshes beyond the sea wall.

High overhead, fieldfares were passing, sweeping forward, not with steady wing-beats, but flying jerkily like all the thrushes, with a few hurried strokes and then setting their wings so that they swooped downwards and upwards in a continuous curve. Some arrested their flight and dived down with closed wings to the tops of the lime avenue by Mellons Platt, for they had just come in and were tired after their long journey across the sea. The fields round about were alive with redwings and fieldfares and many other newly arrived migrants such as starlings and wood-pigeons; here and there curlew stalked amongst them and the green plovers ran.

Manka, having finished his toilet, hissed at a gander that wandered too close, causing him to jump away with a little side-ways hop. Then he began to feed, plucking at the short green blades. A tiny, black knob was bobbing along the far hedge that marked the road. It stopped and Manka's eye caught it. He raised his head and uttered the alarm, quee! quee! Every goose ceased to feed. They all stood at strict attention with necks held very straight, all were focussing on that distant black knob. Foxy pulled a battered pair of field glasses from his pocket (he had picked them up on the marsh five years before) and focussed on the far spots that dotted the big field. His heart gave a bump when he saw the white form of Manka. The bird looked royal in the pale winter sunlight, he could see every feather.

Towards midday the sun dimmed and the wires along the sea wall began to shrill. The change that the shepherd had foretold was coming, snow was already on its way. That evening, when the geese went back to the sea, there was a skin of ice in the cattle "pocks" around the gateways, and the marshes were full of snow buntings. A fog came in on the tide and tweeting pipits were lost as soon as they rose from the herbage of the marsh. A loneliness came with it, a loneliness that is peculiar to this coast. Gunners out on the marsh came back to the bank before their bearings were blotted out, and waited there for the evening flight. It is not pleasant to be far out on the muds when the mists come down, especially if you are a stranger to the coast. From the sea came the trumpeting of ships' sirens as they moved like nervous elephants through the murk. The low sun became a red, faint disc as it sank below the level sands, darkness came quickly from the sea.

Billy blew on his fingers as he stumped back to his cottage.

He met the bailiff by the trestle bridge, a squat, red toad of a man with a bad-tempered face. "Frost comin', Billy!"

"Ah!"

The cattle about the gateways blew tufts of steam from their nostrils, snipe "scaaped" up the little ditches, fringed now with yellow reeds.

Up the marshes flew a wide-winged bird, silently and owl-like, a marsh harrier from the distant broads. Flap, flap-glide, it passed up the foot of the bank. The pipits and snow-buntings cowered in the roots of the sea lavender until the fog had long swallowed up the sinister form with its white barred tail.

Out on the sandbanks the geese were restless, for the fog blinded sight and muffled hearing. They slept fitfully, gabbling loudly among themselves. The tide was moving sluggishly up the gullies and the creeks were filling like a bath. "Krank!" a heron passed over in the half darkness, bound for the wide sands, where he would pass the night wriggling his neck to digest the eels he had swallowed. The body of a dunlin floated past the sand bar; it had been dead three days, shot by a "shore popper" on the other side of the Wash. A black-backed gull had hollowed its body, it was mere shell, to which feathers still adhered. It bumped against the sand bar and grounded. The lipping tide edged it off and it moved on towards the marsh. Other things came past, lumps of seaweed and an empty orange box. The latter caused Manka to croak in alarm, but when he saw it was a lifeless thing, his head sank once more into his shoulders. There was an outburst of gull cries to the south, something had disturbed them. The sound became loud and then died away and only a big gull laughed mockingly far out on the sands.

Very soon some startled wigeon came past, they flew with swiftness, silently, after them a smoke of waders. Around the sand bar the tide hissed and gurgled. It moved over the dry sand at a slow walking pace, and the sea-worm holes bubbled joyfully, sending chains of silver wavering into the deepening water. Manka slept.

Towards midnight the fog began to thin, and a pale disc that was the rising moon hung like a pallid face in the dissolving walls of white. Faint shadows were traced from the sleeping geese. The tide was still making.

Something that was not a log was coming up from the shadow of the land. It was a long, rakish craft with only an inch or two of free board, at its snout the muzzle of a gun wagged wickedly. Foxy was lying full length in the bottom of the boat, kicking the punt along with deft strokes of the hand paddles. The tide bore him gently as it had borne the body of the dunlin.

So well was the man acquainted with this coast that despite the poor visibility he knew exactly where he was. Out of nothingness, into nothingness, yet he pointed the nose of the punt towards the sand bar as if it had been broad daylight and the visibility clear.

The tide rose, lipping creamily towards the geese with never a backward suck. Foxy could hear the nervous trembling pipes of the dunlins and the louder, more hysterical, peeps of the pied oystercatchers that were retreating along the edge of the water. They seemed afraid of getting their feet wet, and when it eventually flooded them off the sand they would pass on down the coast in little bunches, calling to one another, to rest on the high marsh until the tide fell again and exposed a newly spread breakfast table. For to the wildfowl the moonlight nights are as busy as the day, they seldom slept, the tides governed their sleep.

Now and again there was a velvety slurring from under the punt as she touched bottom, once she grounded. Foxy waited until he felt the craft afloat again, for the water was still rising. From out of the murk the twittering grew in volume and then, quite close, he heard the single croak of a goose. Somewhere ahead he knew they

Foxy

were resting on the banks, but the mist still lay just above the water hiding everything, though overhead stars shone and the moon was clear.

Then, as the tide pushed him forwards, round, grey blobs appeared through the mist, and at that instant the sweet silence of night was broken, as a bottle is smashed against a wall. Hell broke loose. Manka, always watchful, and unsleeping since the startled rush of wigeon that had passed a short while ago, saw the dim shape of the punt. He did not know what it was, but his low croak awoke an old goose on the outskirts of the flock. She knew instantly that death was on them, and in a moment all the geese, on a sudden impulse, sprang into the air. The mist was a whirl of big, flapping wings and cacklings, all the geese were skimming away low across the sand. Foxy's fang bit into his lower lip and with a savage pull he yanked the lanyard of the big gun. BOOMP!

Across the bar a singing cloud of BB shot went whistling like bees, three feet above the sand. The punt shot backwards, rocking in a furl of water, a trickle of sinister blue smoke rising from the mouth of the gun. Foxy's eyes were blinded by the flash and in his ears a hundred mosquitoes seemed to be singing.

The air was so moist the smoke hung in a dense cloud (Foxy did not use the best of powder) and for a moment or two he could not guess the result of his shot.

Yet it had been deadly carnage. All around Manka geese had slumped to earth, some never to move, others to flap wildly and struggle as with an invisible foe. Others fled across the sand running with considerable speed, yet others rose raggedly into the air to drop with a splash out in the shallow water.

The geese scattered in all directions, calling wildly to one another. Five turned back over Foxy's head and he downed another with the cripple-stopper (the shot-gun a puntsman always carries in the punt to finish off wounded birds).

Ahead of him he heard scufflings on the sand, wings beating water, hoarse cackles. He jumped out of the punt and ran across the bar, knocking those geese on the head which showed any sign of life. With the cripple-stopper he shot two more that were swimming, strongly, on the tide. The sweat rolled down his chin, despite the cold night, and in a few moments he had collected a pile of nine geese which he carried in several journeys back to the punt.

One skulking goose he lost in the mist, he heard it "hirpling" across the sea, its wing had only been tipped and it was a hopeless task to try and trace it until the fog lifted completely.

He little knew how close he had been to bagging the white goose, one big pellet had actually passed through Manka's tail and another grazed his breast.

Manka was now high above the Wash, calling to his companions. The skein came together and falling into formation, went right out to sea.

Foxy went back to the punt and sat down, lighting his pipe. He would enjoy a quiet smoke before the tide turned. There was silence once more, all the sand bars were empty of geese for miles, for the gigantic explosion had driven them all away, even the waders had gone and Foxy was in full command of the coast, a solitary, contented figure.

There was little fog now and the lights of Boston began to wink clearly to the North. It was a calm and perfect night of broad moonlight, far peeps of the waders, and curlew whistles. Foxy felt very pleased with life in general, the punt was quite low in the water with the weight of the geese in the forepeak.

In the creeks the tide slid to a standstill, cakes of froth wavered to and fro at the mercy of every passing breath.

And then it began to move, at first almost imperceptibly, back towards the open sea. Foxy took up his paddles and pushed off, turning the nose of the punt towards the land.

In the queer light of the moon his shadow was thrown on the bottom boards of the punt, and there was no sound but the quiet dip of his paddles. Now and then, as he drew at his pipe, a reddish glow illuminated his eager, strained face. Soon he saw the dim outlines of the mill against the greenish sky and the masts of the little dinghies rising like a spinney of bare ash poles against the stars.

No light shone in the cottages, everyone was asleep. Only a large owl was perched on top of the mill roof, turning its big head from side to side.

Man and punt were lost for a moment in the shadow of the old warehouse, and secret clinking and sloshings told of disembarkation. For Foxy it had been a good night, and the fifty odd pounds of goose flesh was a pleasant weight. Frost sparkled on the rim of the jetty timbers when he tied up the punt, and as he went down the silent village street, staggering under his load, ice crackled underfoot.

When the geese went back to the fields next day they found the ground iron-hard with frost. As the Lincolnshire geese feed chiefly on potatoes and young wheat, hard weather drives them away, and that night Manka left the Wash with the rest of the skein and headed north. They were led by the same gander that had piloted them from Spitzbergen. Manka was content, as far as he was concerned, to be guided like the rest, for being yet a youngster and unmated, he had not aspired to the true leadership of the skein.

All night they flew in clear starlight, lonely beings in a world of stars. They drove through the night, gaggling to one another a wild song. After the rich fare of the past few weeks they were fit and well, but they had left behind over thirty of their comrades on those bleak fenlands.

Below them glowed furnaces and the clustering constellations of big cities, they passed a lone aeroplane droning through the emptiness of space with a light glowing in its tail, this made them scatter and gaggle in alarm.

Trains, like golden worms, were left far behind and far below, as were the searchlights of the cars speeding along the roads. Below them passed rivers and ships, harbours and mean streets, where picture-palaces were pricked out in many coloured lights, and loungers tarried at grimy street corners.

Before the first hint of dawn was flushing the eastern sky the geese had passed Carlisle and they saw the silver expanse of the Solway below them. Foxy was left behind, nine geese were stiff and stark in his little outhouse on the sea bank, each with a bead of frozen moisture at the end of its pink-banded bill.

But Manka and the rest were still alive and free, setting their wings in a long glide that would take them down to this new world below them.

On the grey-green marshes of Lochar side they came to rest, and their unwearied wings folded after a journey of four hundred odd miles. Here was a new world from the flat fenlands. The air was keener, and mixed with the tang of salt water was the damp, aromatic smell of bracken and heather and peaty water, the essence of the hills. The marshes were not intersected by so many winding gullies, what gullies there were seemed wider and deeper, edged with quaking sand. And on the surface of the marsh, where sweet grass grew, numerous shallow wide pans glimmered in the dawn light, some the size of hip baths, others as big as horse ponds, all full to the brim with salt water.

Snow flakes came wandering in the dawn over Lochar, and one by one the lights of Silloth snuffed out across the silver plain of the Solway. Seven greylag geese rose from the edge of the river and went away towards the hills that now were becoming clear-cut to the North, whitened about their tops with fresh fallen snow. Along the edge of the tide was a regiment of pied geese as vivid in colouring as magpies. They were barnacle geese, rare stragglers to the fenlands, but common enough on Solwayside. They were considerably smaller than the pink-feet, with ungooselike faces and tiny, insignificant bills. When they fed they cooed like doves, and like the doves were gentle creatures, easily brought down by small shot. They fed on the marsh grass and very rarely ventured off, they were not inland feeders like the grey geese. Most of their gazing was done at night, for it was risky during the day, the marshes were alive with gunners at this season.

Most of the young pink-feet in Manka's skein had never seen barnacles before, they were almost unknown in the region of the Esker bluffs.

The leader of the skein knew this country well. For twenty winters he had come here, and he knew every creek and gully. He also knew the feeding grounds inland and the remote lochs in the hills where they were never disturbed.

For the next three weeks they remained in the district, resting at night on the sandbanks off Lochar mouth and flighting in to the fields to feed. On the other side of the Solway, on the Rock-cliffe marshes, were thousands of other pinks, but for some reason the old gander of Manka's skein rarely went over the water. Perhaps he had had some narrow escape there years before.

One day, when the geese were resting at midday on the marshes by East Park, a great tide swept the grey-green expanse. Backed by a high westerly gale it came roaring in across the acres of sand in a white wall. Soon it was shooting up into the air at the foot of the high merse in white plumes, the spray falling forward in a moving sheet.

Rapidly the gullies filled and Lochar became as broad as the Danube. Three gunners, crouched in the whins along the point of marsh, saw a wonderful sight.

In a very short space the sea was breaking on to the high merse (as the marsh is termed in Scotland) and sheep, feeding on the merse itself, were cut off by the fast rising water. They ran wildly about when they found they were trapped, the water lapping their bellies.

Soon they were swimming, one by one they rolled over, exhausted, to float away like grey barrels on the waves. Poor little hares, likewise trapped, swam gallantly; one reached a small island of grass and whins where it crouched miserably, like a half-drowned mouse, to be engulfed by the waves.

The grey geese took the air and went away up the coast to the dark line of woods that marked Caerlaverock Castle, half hidden in the driving rods of grey rain. The gunners watched them go and cursed, for they had hoped the tide would drive them within shot of the whin bushes where they lay in hiding, and the white goose would have indeed been a prize. They had to retreat and only got back to the mainland with a severe wetting.

As quickly as it had arisen the water dropped, leaving sackfulls of dead hares and a dozen or more drowned sheep lying on the sodden grass.

On calm, starlit nights, when the tide was low, and the frost glittered on the sea wrack, Manka would hear the barnacle geese in full cry up the edge of the tide, a sound that was like the yapping of puppies. And the big greylag geese, who weighed three or four pounds more than the "pinks," answered hoarsely from the sands.

The clear morning sun was shining on the white-capped Sidlaws, the frosty air smelt like new-cut hay.

Across the Tay the sky was clear, fresh minted with full dawn, the river bright with its reflected glory. A sharp frost overnight had partly frozen the foreshore leaving cakes of ice along the edge of the tide. The sun sparkled on the shorter roots of the reeds that grew in stubbly spikes out of the iron-bound muds. Little skins of ice, like white napkins, were suspended from root tip to root tip— the frozen sea water, which left a film balanced on the reed stubbles as it receded.

Carrion crows flew up and down the river cawing one to

another, and in the middle of the Tay a party of greylag geese were cackling hoarsely.

Between the hills and river lay the Carse of Gowrie, a rich and fertile land, as rich as those dark fenland meadows that stretch around the Wash. Like those Lincolnshire fields, many farms were studded about, and on the Carse the wildfowl from the river found food and sanctuary. As it was all private land, the shooting was private also, and the geese were left in peace. Only along the river, where the local fowlers plied their punts, did danger lurk.

For hundreds of years the geese had come to the Carse, to find good pasturage and peace. Manka was sitting on a sandbank off Mugdrum Island. They had come overnight from Solwayside and because of their journey they were hungry.

Northwards, as he stood on the sand bar, he could see the Sidlaws, rich lands beyond, as rich as the Carse itself, between the Sidlaws and the Grampians.

Manka climbed with the skein of fifteen pink-feet in the clear sunlight, and the Carse, woods and farms fell away below and dwindled. He could see eastwards the reek of Dundee, to the west the smoke of Perth, and as they climbed still higher, far Edinburgh and Glasgow, the latter a smudge of yellow fog away to the south. Behind them the sea sparkled in the sun, the Eden was a silver snake beyond Tay bridge.

Manka, near the head of the skein, shone as white as the snow-capped mountains before him. The air was cutting cold, with a razor keenness. The woods appeared purple, the beech woods copper gold, for the leaves had fallen and still lay beneath the bare trees. They were heading for a nick in the hills before them and after a while the ground began to slope to meet them, the woods became sharper, the details of the countryside more clear. Manka could see the farms with their neat rows of small straw stacks ranged within their trim yards, each with a pool of shadow beside them, and a train puffing slowly along the Carse, leaving a trail of white smoke that drifted with a shadow and melted like snow. Nearer and ever nearer came the hills, now the trees were in vivid detail, the roads that wound between the woods, the parks and plantations where pheasants dotted the green policies.

And as the land rose the geese rose, the cleft passed beneath them, and before lay the misty and fertile valley hemmed in by the far Grampian range. Before them now was no barrier, the ground fell rapidly away into a bowl of mist, the geese had no need to gain altitude.

It was a wonderful sight to anyone who chanced to be watching that morning flight of the grey wild geese. For behind Manka's band came others, skein after skein, some in small parties, others in long lines hundreds strong, rising like files of infantry coming to attack, over the white-capped Sidlaws.

And now the geese set their wings, the labour (though it was not labour to them) of flying was over, they could let the air take them down the long incline. With sweet ease of motion they sped downwards, calling one to another in wild and joyful voices, sped downwards in a glide that took them six miles or more. Now and then with a skilful twist of a pinion they altered course, there were many fields they knew and loved, but on some were sheep and on others men.

They came to rest on a little L-shaped meadow, remote and far from any road. It has been the feeding-ground of wild geese from time immemorial and here they were protected by a farmer who studied wild birds and kept sanctuary for them. Some years this field was sown with wheat, but the grain did not thrive, the ground was too moist. In one corner was a large flood flash which the geese used for washing and drinking, and this was perhaps why the ground was so much sought after. Round the edge of the flash were white feathers, and a crowd of peewits happily splashed and rollicked in the shallow water.

Five fields away, carts were moving like slugs across a field, and

"Over the white-capped Sidlaws"

a man was pulling manure with a long-pronged fork, scattering it about the stubble. He was a tall, spare man, this grieve, all his life he had lived in the district. He heard the cry of the geese and saw the wheeling skein, but hardly turned his head. He saw them light below the forest of little fence-posts and then, as it was eleven-thirty, he put down his fork and tramped back to the farm. Other labourers were likewise going home for lunch, the fields were dotted with the toiling figures, and the ice in the cart ruts starred and cracked under their hobnailed boots.

The geese fed in this same field for over a week. Sometimes aeroplanes would send them clamouring skywards, but otherwise they were not disturbed. With long usage the pasture became fouled, and when this was the case the geese moved to other favourite fields in the locality.

Though it took a man some hours to reach the river over the mountains the geese did the journey in a few minutes. That far nick in the hills was their guide and whenever they flighted back to the water they held their course for this mark. In the afternoons, when they had had their fill of sweet grass they rose in clamouring lines, passing over the hills in waving ribbons, calling one to another a thousand feet above the Carse.

By the river the tall reeds, ten feet high and more, formed a dense screen. They grew so thick in places, and had done so for generations, that even a dog could not force a passage through them. Old reeds, long used, rotted down, falling all ways and forming a criss-cross barrier, and through them rose the new slender rods, tough and strong. In the winter the reed cutters came and cut wide lanes and swathes with their sharp hooks. The reeds were used for thatching. This industry was a very old one, and the Tay reeds were famed for durability and toughness.

The reed cutters often saw Manka as they worked in the frosty sunlight.

In these reed forests the shy water rail lived, a quaint little bird which uneducated people would identify as a moorhen, for it had the same sooty plumage and white undertail coverts. But its bill was long and curved, redder than a withered reed. Occasionally, marsh harriers came beating up the reeds, turning their fierce eyes this way and that, searching for voles and mice.

And sometimes, in the autumn, an occasional caper would come out of the fir woods across the Carse, Rob the fowler had shot a number in the reeds.

On quiet nights, when the moon was young, the pinks and greys fed among these reeds, not the tall reeds, but the short stubbles that had been worn by the tide, or where the reed cutters had been at work.

Then there was such a gabbling and a tearing, such a chasing and a fighting that the sound could be heard for a long distance, and men might stalk them and even crawl right amongst them when the wind rustled the taller reed beds.

The big greylag geese, the ancestors of our domestic geese, lived mostly in the river. Sometimes they flighted in to graze on the fields close to the river, and they never, like the pinks, crossed the Sidlaws to the Carse beyond. Why, no men knew. Though they appeared stupid big birds and the fowlers had it that they were more easily decoyed than any of the geese, they were perhaps more wary than the pinks, and on the river very few were shot.

Among the reeds, the geese fed on the knobby, hard rootlets which looked not unlike potatoes, and to the pink-feet this formed a variety of fare. All the greys fed at night, and only during the new moon did the pinks feed in the reeds.

Many a night Manka heard the rumbling of the trains as they crossed the Tay bridge, and saw the chain of tiny lights wending their way from shore to shore. The smoke from the engines drifted over the mother o' pearl mud flats. With the changing sky the mud changed, pink with the sunset, saffron with the dawn, blue in the winter sunlight and grey in the winter days.

The eternal tides lulled the resting geese on the sand bars and, as dusk deepened, the lights of Dundee and Perth danced the firefly dance.

Sometimes Manka flew to Montrose basin, a shining dish beyond Lunan Bay, where in summertime the blue sea creams across the golden gull-painted sands.

The cold winds of winter tempered, already on the hills the snow dwindled daily and the moorfolk, the blackcock and the grouse, crowed with greater exuberance at break o' day.

The geese went back to Solway at the end of March and then to Solway Moss, where great gatherings of geese assembled daily, talking over the journey that lay before them.

The evenings lengthened and from the hill farms came the bleat of lambs. Solway Moss was a forbidding place, swampy heath lands dark and peaty, with little birch groves, a wild and broken country where the Lost Legion somewhere sleeps its last sleep. More and more geese dribbled in from the south, and then once again, they moved back to the Tay district, which is one of the "jumping" places for migrating geese.

For Manka and the skeins the new urge was daily stronger, almost a fever, and as the shooting season was over, they grew brazen, feeding sometimes close to roads. The birches were already a tender green, the burns turbulent with melted snow water, yet still they lingered. Unlike the swallows, who had the equinoctial gales to fear, the geese could afford to wait, and those early days of spring coming to the hills were pleasant after winter frosts and hard days. There was a new song too in the reeds, not the dry, shivering rustle of starved and dead vegetation. The curlews had left the coast for their breeding quarters on the moors, and with them went the trim-spangled plovers and redshanks from the tidal oozes. One day three swallows came hawking over the reeds, twittering with happiness and joy that England was theirs once more. Parties of geese were already beginning to leave, every day there were fewer on the Carse. They departed at night, secretly and without fuss, and one morning in early April the white goose and his companions did not take their usual flight out to the Sidlaws. Six thousand feet above the earth, they were on their way to Spitz-bergen, and no man saw them go. They were in the van of the great army of feathered spirits, all drawn by a common instinct to the land of their birth.

Those great caravan routes of the sky are clearly mapped, and in spring and autumn how busy those highways become!

Far behind Manka lay the rich fields of the Carse, the mountains, the wild glens and rivers where the silver salmon ran, far behind lay the flat lands of the Wash where Foxy lived his lowly life. At that moment Foxy was leaning over the trestle bridge, spitting into the tide. From the big ploughed field behind Mellons Platt gulls were mewing in the wake of a ploughman.

There was a white feather caught in the dead stubble. The bright share swept it under the breast of the plough. Rich, dark earth fell gently over and the feather was hidden—Manka's feather, dropped on Leader's Drove five months before.

Chapter Five
THE SECOND WINTER

Inchgarvie is far from any road. It is a field, a big field, hidden away behind a forest of fences at the foot of the hills. In winter those hills are mostly white, their tops mysterious and wreathed in constant vapour. But sometimes on clear evenings they are hard edged, blue-grey; waiting for the frost.

A MAN, sitting in a dentist's chair in a grimy northern city, was looking through the grimy window at the leaden sky. What he saw was a brick wall and the top of a starved almond tree where sparrows were holding parliament. Above the brick wall was the upper half of a factory chimney, smokeless, and as weathered as a mountain.

The dentist had gone out of the surgery to await the numbing of the cocaine in his victim's gum.

He was alone with his own sorrows and apprehensions, listening with awful expectancy for the sound of returning steps, his heart quailing at the thought of deftly inserted forceps, produced from behind the dentist's back.

He felt a condemned man, trapped, his mind went roving on his own life, a grey life lived amidst pavements, smoke, and poverty.

We see him sitting there and feel a detachment, we are not bothered with what he is or what he does, he is of no account, he does not play any part in this book. This poor little man is necessary to the story because he shows the meanness of some men's lives, of most men's lives.

With quiet misery he looked at the autumn sky, at the brick wall, at the free sparrows. And then, across the murky clouds, from behind the weathered stack of the chimney, a skein of geese came in sight. They were in arrow formation, the foremost bird showed white against the background. They were high, hardly visible. In a minute they had passed behind the jamb of the window and were gone. Manka was flying South, was coming home after the short Arctic summer, he was coming back as the swallow returns to its rafter in the barn.

The man in the chair groaned, he knew not why, and then he heard the steps of the dentist returning.

Manka was flying South for another winter in the fields, by lonely steading and highland tarn, for more journeyings by starlight and sunlight, for more escapes, for new delights, for the sound of the wind on the marshes, for the rushing tides. He was coming for those silent frostbound nights, when the moonlight holds the world in a deathly pallor, for the soft, mild days when the thrushes sing, for the whirling snowflake in lonely places where no man sees or comes.

The man in the chair heard a movement behind him, his hour had come. With forced bravado he said, "I've just seen a lot of ducks flying over there, behind the chimney; migrating, I suppose. Wonderful thing migration, you know."

"Ah, so I understand . . . now open wide, please; I won't hurt you."

The little man "opened wide."

Inchgarvie is far from any road. It is a field, a big field, hidden away behind a forest of fences at the foot of the hills. In winter those hills are mostly white, their tops mysterious, wreathed in constant vapour. Though not always, for on clear evenings they sometimes are clear cut, waiting for the frost. In the dark pinewoods that clothe the lower slopes live great capers. They are seldom seen, and higher still above the snowline, the snowbuntings flit from stone to weathered stone, white spirits of the Snow Queen.

Sometimes sheep graze on Inchgarvie, sometimes it is clear of stock all winter through. On moonlight nights the geese come in, clamouring one to another, calling for guidance, and home-going grieves and labourers look upwards and see the waving scarves holding high against the stars.

Manka's first feed of the winter was often on Inchgarvie, and now on this November night, he was bringing his skein down. The moon was clear, though over the mountains massed white clouds came like herds of little silent sheep, filmy blobs that dimmed the radiance of the moon.

"Brrrrrrrrrrrrrrr," sang the wind in Manka's strong pinions as he tipped sideways and threw himself down on to Inchgarvie.

It was quiet then as the geese listened and looked. Not far away was a black barn, strangely reminiscent of Starvation Point, with the silhouette of a horse's head hanging out of it, drooped in sleep.

A crested peewit ran among the tussocks and said "Pee Wee." "Peep," replied a golden plover, for there was a pack of the round-shouldered little birds feeding on Inchgarvie.

When the tide flooded them off the bars these birds went off in a great hurry, together with drab dunlin sprites, heads down, shoulders bent to the task, all hurrying along the water's edge.

Feeding was good in Inchgarvie, for many years the river fowl found fine fare among its tussocks. Other geese had gone using the field, pinks, on their journey south. The droppings were all over the field, little piles of dung where geese had been to sleep sitting down.

Manka was like a fairy prince in the moonlight, white against the drab tones of the sward, his shadow black in contrast. They fed, plucking up the sweet roots greedily, and when full fed, sitting down and feeling for fleas.

A car passed along the Garvie road, a moving ray of bright light, and Manka's eye caught it and watched it go. Harmless things, cars.

In the next meadow sheep bleated and moved about in the

darkness. How sweet to rest here after the ceaseless beating of wings!

"Anka, anka!" Far away a lost single pinkfoot was calling, the sound died away and away over the lonely hills.

There was a mallard in the burn on the other side of the field. Every now and then he felt so pleased with the quiet night he rose on his toes and proclaimed "Quar, quar, quar!" There were other ducks higher up the burn, all feeding in the blessed quiet of night.

Manka preened carefully, feeling gently with his bill among the broad feathers that meant life and freedom to him. He was full of sweet grass and felt sleepy. Another feeding goose came too near; he stretched his neck and hissed. Manka got up and ran at him and then sat down again.

The cities slept, on the roads the traffic melted like snow. This was Manka's world. The sky was his, the fields were his, the stars, the moon, the winds.

Among his skein were a great many young birds who had not come to Britain before. They were two and three pounds less in weight than Manka, and the cliffs of Spitzbergen were still part of them and in their minds. They did not yet understand, as Manka, in the long ago, had not understood, these quiet croftings and sweet-smelling grass; none had learnt of man and the bang and sting of guns. Some would fall easy prey to the longshore fowlers, most would wander off in little parties away from the main skein. And always there was a shuffling of numbers. Sometimes, after these autumn migrations, the big skeins would split up, and Manka had as few as ten companions.

Dawn came over the river mists, and with the light, filmy clouds drove away South, leaving a clear, cold sky. Then Manka lifted and went away to the river and the geese shouted to one another as they went above the fowler's house on Inchgarvie burn. He heard them, and going to the window, saw the skein passing over for the river.

Rob, the fowler, saw Manka, and he pulled at his pipe as he watched him go over Macdonald's farm with its row of neat haystacks and the tall grey silo.

Rob lived alone with his old spaniel Bob. Bob was as good as a wife, Rob always said, sometimes even a little better. Many a good flight had they had together. Maybe Manka was using Inchgarvie, later he would go and see. A white goose was worth shooting.

After breakfast he walked across with Bob and examined the ground. There was no doubt about it, the geese were there in force, and it might be worth a visit. He went at four that afternoon, just before high water. There was frost on the field, it crusted every grass blade, and even the droppings were frozen.

The sky in the west was red, the mountains clear of cloud. Rob and Bob lay down by the burn and waited for dusk. The sound of the water was soothing, full of trout, musical at every shillet. The sky grew dark, and golden plover came piping in.

Rob went on to the field, and pulling his coat round him, sat down, Bob beside him. The dog was listening intently. Sometimes when a starling passed, the spaniel crouched and then looked foolish. Rob had many a laugh over his dog. Sometimes he had watched him duck his head at a gnat.

The red in the West died and smouldered, there was nothing but the faint talk of the burn behind the line of alders that fringed the bank. Rob could see the tall silo on Macdonald's farm rising above the field mists, and a mallard whistled over. The black mass of the barn on Inchgarvie became a blur, melting into the background of trees, the fences melted too, dusk had come.

"Hist, Bob!" breathed the fowler, and the dog, which had heard the geese before Rob, flattened, nose to ground. A party was coming off the river, for the tide had lifted them. They passed in a long smoky ribbon across the stars and dipped behind Inchgarvie farm.

More parties came, some holding for the hills, a single goose set its wings and pitched in a field not far away and was immediately one with its surroundings.

In the Codoon woods (Sir Brian Macnab's place, where the caper lived) owls hooted, far away an engine whistled.

Rob and Bob, sitting on the field, melted like the shed and fences until all was a duskiness.

"Anka! anka!" more geese coming. Rob saw them soon, holding high above Inchgarvie, and he saw the white form of Manka, as white as a barn owl, leading the skein.

The dog lay quivering as the safety-catch on his master's gun clicked. But Manka was not coming in, he was holding for the hills.

Rob took from his pocket the wooden goose call on which he could imitate the call of a lost gander to perfection. He sounded it as the moose-hunter sounds his birch-bark horn. But once geese have made up their mind where they are going, nothing will turn them, and Manka was heading for the V cut in the hill where a star hung and beckoned.

Man and dog lay long on the field, and when the moon was up two hours, they went away to the fireside and the little brick cottage, where Rob got out his box of butterflies that he had collected himself around the district and Bob caught fleas—or pretended to catch them—stretched on the hearth-rug.

After Manka and fifteen of his companions had been in the Inchgarvie district for a week (sometimes dropping into the field where Rob waited that night, sometimes using other less loved fields in the Carse) a great frost came with the full of the moon. The marshes, the reed-beds, were turned into a fairy land and the world seemed made of iced sugar. Down on the foreshore the stubbly short spikes of the old tideworn reeds were coated with crusted icicles so that they seemed to be fairy chandeliers. The tides piled up the floes along the water's edge and, when the tide was flowing, squares of ice turned over and up, catching the rays of the moon. This moonlight also made the marsh a treasure store of diamonds, and Rob, walking across the Inchgarvie burn was dazzled with the pricking, furtive lights; the ground seemed strewn with precious stones.

Out in the river the muds, bared by the tides, froze solid so that they would bear the weight of a man with ease, and only where the burns ran in was the mud soft. Here the little jack snipe and his cousin the full came to quest about. Just at dusk the greylags came into the burnsides to feed among the reeds.

But to attempt to stalk a goose on the edge of the reeds was a hopeless task. Rob made as much noise as if he were walking through cucumber frames, and the sharp edges of ice cut the dog's feet.

The geese, frozen out over the hills, came back in force to the Carse, where the sea winds subdued the sting of the frost and Inchgarvie was once again alive with geese under the full moon.

Rob shot seven one night, and next morning, in the light of the clear and frosty sun, he found two more birds lying a field away, close to some grazing horses; they were young birds of the year, hatched on the Esker Bluffs.

It is dangerous for geese to form regular habits. If they use a field too long the grieve tips the word to his gunner friends, for the pasture is damaged and sheep do not like fouled ground.

Manka and his companions, starved out from over the mountains came nightly to Inchgarvie, and Rob was in an ace of shooting the white goose one night. But Manka seemed to bear a charmed life. It was a peewit that saved him, for it rose keening at the dark form crouched behind a fencing post. The sudden alarm note turned Manka, who was gliding in with set wings within eighty yards of the fowler. Rob fired as the white goose turned, but the range was too great and the heavy shot never cut a feather.

Manka was too wise a goose to use Inchgarvie for long, and a week before Christmas he found another farm at the edge of the

Carse, just where the first swelling of the ground rose to embrace the Sidlaws. The farmer had gone bankrupt and much of the harvest had been left on the fields. The rotting corn had been piled in "cauls," and after the grass-feed the grain was a welcome and delicious change. Moreover, this farm was rarely shot over. The shooting was leased to a rich jute importer in Dundee and he did not bother with the geese; partridges, hares and pheasants (the latter from the Codoon woods) were more to his liking, so the geese fed in peace. Knowing by instinct their security, they fed with brazen impudence in the sunny days that followed with the thaw, and they waxed fat on the rich corn fare. But Manka was ever on the watch. It was always Manka that stood sentry, and one day Rob, passing along the Codoon road with Bob in the pannier strapped to the carrier of his motor-bike, saw a white blob sitting on top of a caul. He stopped his machine and looked at the blob through his glasses and saw a sight that made him smile. Feeding among the strewn corn about the foot of the caul were ten to fifteen pinks, some sitting with intucked heads, sleeping, others sitting also, but lazily plucking at the corn about them, too full-fed to get up and hunt around. And right on top of the caul stood Manka, his long neck straight up, the sharp little eyes scanning the countryside. The sun was shining on the white form and through the glass Rob could see every detail of the splendid bird.

The geese were quite unstalkable as long as Manka remained at his post, and Rob marvelled at the sagacity of geese in general. Every day until the new year the geese used this field, and very often the big "greys" from the river joined them and fed with them, but always there was a sentry on the watch, though only Manka climbed the caul.

Then came days of dense fog when the ships' sirens sounded from beyond the Tay bridge, and the geese wandered calling through the murk, dangerous days for geese, for the mist cloaked hidden perils and they knew not where they were. And so Manka, uneasy, fighting fit from the rich Carse fare, took his skein away South, and when at last the foggy days had gone, and with the moon coming to the full, more frost silvered the Carse, the white form was no longer seen there. Only the big greys used the corn-field, and the Carse was empty of pinks.

In those silent frosty nights Rob lay in the reeds watching the lights on the Tay bridge winking in the blue-green moonlight and heard the rumble of trains crossing the river. He saw the shooting stars falling over the glare of Dundee and Perth but the geese had gone and no baying of whist hounds was heard. Manka was back on the Wash, back to the familiar fields that had not known him for a year, back to Foxy, the rabbit-toothed Foxy, who knew of the white goose's arrival within twenty hours.

Two miles from the Shardwaners' farm and within a mile of Leader's Drove there was a small farm called Willowhills. It was reached by a narrow rutty lane, miry in winter-time and full of shining puddles, flanked on either hand by the inevitable dykes, in which grew tall and slender reed wands that were for ever shivering. North of the farm were seven leaning willow trees that grew round a little horse-pond. Their red roots felt their way down into the black water like bundles of fingers. The country lads had it that huge carp inhabited the sinister depths, but no fish was ever caught there.

Behind the farm was a wired-in enclosure, built round another smaller pond, and here Mr. Comfrey, the owner of the farm, kept his wildfowl. Comfrey was quite a renowned student of bird life. Professors had been known to consult him upon various species of wildfowl. He had collected all the birds himself. There were two barnacle geese from the Solway, six greylags, five pinks, and a single brent goose that had been caught in the nets set out on the muds of the Wash.

Besides the geese, he had a fine variety of ducks, pintails, pochards, wigeon, and mallard, all either reared within the enclosure, or birds that had been brought to him by the longshore fowlers, "tipped" birds, that is, geese or duck that had been wounded in the wings and deprived of the power of flight.

Every winter the gunners on the outmarsh shot several geese in this way (by mistake, of course), and they were always taken along to Willowhills. A live bird fetched more than a dead one, and the fowlers were glad of a few extra shillings.

Wildfowl, and especially wild geese, were Comfrey's great interest in life, he collected them as other men collect eggs or stamps. And he looked after them too. The pen was large and covered a quarter of an acre. At one end were orchard trees that gave shade in summer to sleeping waterfowl.

Comfrey took immense pride in showing them to any stranger who happened to be interested and would talk for hours about hybrids and freak fowl.

"Geese are strange birds," he would say, wagging his head. "I like the ducks, mind you, and there's few ducks can beat a wigeon, a cock wigeon in winter plumage. But it's the geese that interest me. I look for them in the autumn and am sorry when they go in the spring. The summer's a dull time for me. Then I come out here and watch my birds."

And he would recount past days, good days, on the marshes. Once he and two friends had killed over ninety geese on one of his fields under the moon. "Never again, mister. I've never wanted to shoot a goose since, they're better alive." And what he said was true. Since that night he had never shot another goose.

He did not guess how his captives longed to be free. When they heard their wild companions passing over against the stars they would run up and down the wire, beating their crippled wings and calling. And the wild geese answered, sometimes wheeling round and coming close to the orchard. They saw the long skeins heading North in the spring and felt the dreadful pain for which there was no relief, and in the autumn nights, when the upper skies

"Heading North in the Spring"

were restless and rustling with wings, they cried aloud again. Yet, for the rest of the year, they were content. Wild geese are adaptable creatures and in confinement become very tame. Comfrey looked after them well, and they had plenty of good food; hardship was a thing of the past.

How well they came to know the pen, every yard of it, every loop of wire in the netting. They bathed with the ducks in the pond and in summer-time rested in the shade of the apple trees where the goldfinches sang. There was a little grass in the enclosure but it was kept short by the geese, cropped close as a rabbit pasture.

Comfrey had of course seen Manka many times and talked with the longshore fowlers about him, Foxy in particular. He was talking now in the grey light of a fading afternoon. "My! Foxy, if you could get hold of that white goose for me, it's a fiver for you. A fiver alive, and a couple of quid dead!" Foxy smiled.

"Ah, Mr. Comfrey, now you're askin' summat; I tried to get 'im all last winter. 'E's back now, came in with the others a couple o' days ago."

"Where are they feeding?"

"Mellons Platt, as usual—young Mr. Shardwaner's been after 'im, but there's no one can get nigh 'im, 'e's that wily."

Comfrey knew Shardwaner well. He remembered that in the barn at Willowhills there was a goose-net, and a sudden idea was born. Why not try to catch Manka! It might be done if the geese were using the field regularly.

He went with Foxy up to the barn and from behind a dusty pile of rakes, boxes, and sacks, they pulled the net out. Many of the meshes were torn and the net gaped in big rents, but it could be repaired. With a new spring fitted it might be put into working order. Years ago his father had used it on the fields, and Comfrey remembered the big catches that had been made with it.

It was worth a trial. A wild albino pink-foot would be the pride of his collection, something worth showing. The more he thought of the scheme the keener he became and soon, in his mind, he could already see the white form of Manka bathing in the pond or walking up and down the wire at feeding-time.

"I'll speak to Mr. Shardwaner about it, Foxy. I've a mind he'll let us have a go."

Foxy did not reply. He regarded Manka as his property and he could recall many a bitter dawn (when Comfrey had been tucked up warm in bed) when he had laid in wait out on the marshes, hoping against hope for a shot at the white goose.

But when Comfrey mentioned the matter to young Shardwaner the latter would have none of it, he wanted to shoot the geese in the near future and did not wish them to be disturbed. So the matter was allowed to drop, and though Comfrey had the net repaired, it was put back behind the rakes and the boxes in the corner of the barn and forgotten.

Manka found changes on the marshes. The bombing range had been closed to gunners, and a big white notice-board was set up on the sea-bank. It read, "No wildfowl to be shot on the bombing ranges. Trespassers will be prosecuted. By Order of the Air Ministry."

Not that this notice made any difference to Foxy; he used to go at night and shoot just the same. But it meant peace on the morning flight, and not a shot was fired when the geese came off the sea.

There was a good deal of opposition from the local men who had shot the marshes since they were boys, and their fathers before them. But the official seal of the Government scared them. Years ago the farmers had tried to stop them shooting on the marsh, and had put up notices forbidding people access. But the notices were torn down and the farmers had to acknowledge themselves worsted.

With this new threat came tales of local men who had been caught on the range and had their guns confiscated by a sergeant and two privates with *fixed bayonets*! But they couldn't catch Foxy, the latter was too wily a bird, and only he knew the ways of the tides and every winding creek.

The days passed uneventfully for Manka. The Shardwaners' shoot never came off. After using Leader's Drove for a few days all the geese went away. They moved to Willowhills, and Comfrey's heart beat high with hope. The first morning he saw Manka and thirty others on his winter wheat he fetched out the net again, resolving to let the geese have a "say." He let them alone for two days. But something warned the geese of impending danger, and on the third day they never came. Instead of heading for Willowhills, all the geese crossed the Wash to the Frieston side, and when Comfrey eagerly scanned the wide fields behind the farm he saw only curlew stalking and plovers drilling.

Always there was a shuffling of wildfowl, every week saw fresh arrivals and new departures, mallard coming in from Northern Europe, wigeon by the thousand, others moving North to Scotland and across the sea to Ireland.

Manka wandered too, visiting the Severn and Suffolk marshes, never staying for long in any locality, always on the look-out for guns.

One week he might be at Frieston, another at Holbeach and Long Sutton (where there was a perfect nest of gunners) on another, he might be hundreds of miles away, North or South.

It is this wandering habit of the geese that makes goose chasing such a chancy business, but where they can find good feeding, and are unmolested, they may stay for as long as a week on the same field.

The winter was passing quickly. Fortune had been kind to Manka. Only fourteen of his original skein that came with him from Spitzbergen had been shot, one on Stiffkey freshets, the others on the Suffolk coast and the Tay. He had been fired at several times, but always he was far out of range and did not even alter course.

February came, mild and open after a short spell of hard frost, and Manka came back to the Wash. It would not be long to the gathering of the skeins, for already there were signs of spring. It had been an easy winter, little hard weather and plenty of rich food, and, what was more important, plenty of good luck.

In the second week in February a long, shiny car drew up by the shepherd's cottage and a tall man climbed out.

Foxy, coming along the sea-wall with dog at heel on his way to the morning flight, altered course; these amateur wildfowlers were the curse of his life, and he loathed the sight of them. Every year more of them came and none of them knew the first thing about shooting. All they did was to scare the geese away.

He went along the foot of the bank, intending to cross the fence by the middle level.

"Hey, you, just a moment!"

Foxy pretended not to hear, but trudged on along the foot of the wall.

"I say! You!"

There was the sound of running feet, and Foxy, glowering, turned to see the stranger bearing down upon him. He was clothed in the most extraordinary fashion, a typical "shore-popper" rig-out, thought Foxy. On his head was a flapping balaclava, below, a red polo jersey, and long rubber boots that were "concertinaed" down each leg.

Foxy eyed the creature with distaste, and spat, truculently.

"I say!"—drawling—"I say! I want to shoot a goose, are there any about heah?"

Foxy spat again before replying.

"Ain't seen a goose for over a month; gone clean away some-wheres."

Considering Foxy had shot a goose two nights previously at Horseshoe gull this was hardly true. And had the shore-popper been for the evening flight the day before he would have seen quite a thousand geese going out to the sea.

"There may be one or two back," added Foxy as an after-thought, "but they're as wild as 'awks; you won't get a shot at 'em."

"Well, where's the best place to go?"

"Oh, anywheres over there!" said Foxy, waving vaguely in the direction of the bombing range. "You ain't supposed to goo too far down that way, but if you do they won't say nothing to you."

Foxy directed the man to a place where he had never shot a goose in his life.

"Follow that there crik till you get to the sands, an' you'll find a deep gull. You can get down there, you might get a shot at a curlee bud."

Foxy turned about and swung off across the marshes towards Mudhorse creek. It was a windy morning, and the dawn was greying over the targets to the South.

He reached the creek and unslung his goose bag to make himself a dry seat on the side of the dyke. The wiry, matted stems of the sea-lavender formed a nice springy couch, and he settled down to wait. He took out his pipe and filled it, gazing with satisfaction at the shore-popper, manfully struggling across the marsh towards a creek that did not exist, and falling into deep grips on the way.

Foxy could smell the clean naked breath of the sea, of marshes that have lain all night under the stars, the smell of the muds and the little runnels. He watched the pipits flitting about among the sea-blite and an odd curlew or two going inland. The procession of gulls began to stream across the sky, eastwards it began to flush pink. A wet day by the look of it, thought Foxy.

The distant figure of Foxy's victim was now very small on the sands, searching about and standing, now and then gaping at the sea. Well, if the geese were out there he might put 'em over Foxy. The Twirp!

The "Twirp" found a drain at last. It was not a very big one, but he found that if he curled up he could be tolerably well hidden. He had at least the sense to know that to shoot wildfowl you must hide. His right leg was wet to the waist and he felt rather uncomfortable. But, by Jove! there was something about being out on the marshes like this that was rather grand, don't you know, bit different from town!

He sensed an elemental feeling in the drab expanse of marsh, the piping wind, the crying of the wildfowl. And the wind was rising in the west, it "bluntered" in the ears of his helmet and whistled hollowly in the dead sea-lavender stalks. A redshank came past, wind-tossed, legs hanging and white rump showing. The "Twirp" was a good hand at a woodcock, dodging between the stems of trees, and a deadly shot at pheasants coming over Sussex woods, but he missed this little bird by miles. The redshank let out a shriek of alarm and vanished. The "Twirp" pushed another cartridge into the smoking breech of his Purdey. "Little beggar, wonder what it was; some sort of snipe by the look of it!"

Landwards there was a star shining from Billy's window, and as the "Twirp" watched it the lamp snuffed out. It was quite light now and he could see his surroundings in detail—the sea-wall, the leaning trees, the white greenhouses behind Mellons Platt, the tiny dot of Billy going along the sea-wall. He couldn't see Foxy anywhere, cunning old bird, no doubt; bet he'd shot a good many geese!

He sat watching the continual procession of gulls passing over, some within a few feet of his head, close enough to see their little beady eyes and trim paddles. He raised his gun and shot one, just to get his "eye in." It dropped cleanly and he went out and collected it. Then he felt sorry he had shot it, for it was a harmless common gull. He tossed it into the gully and watched the tide drift the body out of sight up the creek.

Foxy, away in Horseshoe gull, saw the gull fall and cursed afresh, though not from any humanitarian motive. Shots would scare any geese that were resting on the sand and if the "Twirp" was going to start shooting gulls, not a goose or a duck would come within miles.

Landwards Foxy saw moving curtains of rain hiding the distant farms and trees. Day had fully come now and the gulls had ceased their procession overhead. They would be stalking in the rain now, on the shining cheesy furrows. Surprisingly, beyond Mellons Platt, there was a break in the sky, soon the rain would be over, with this wind it could not last for long.

Very soon now these marshes would be green again. How strange it was to think of the spring, of the swallows and the cuckoo, the chattering reed birds in the dykes, the merciless days when the sun shone brazenly in this land of treeless shade. And then the time of the hay, with the sweet wind rippling the mowing grass, the un-tiring "crake, crake" of the corncrakes (they were becoming rarer each year) and then, at last, the autumn.

Foxy had no love for the summer days when the sea was blue and the sands golden, specked with scraps of gulls. There was no shooting then. Odd days of work with farmers at harvest-time and mowing time, odd shillings here and there, work he loathed. Well, it wouldn't be long now, the geese would be gone in a week or two, he wouldn't see Manka again for many a weary month, much might happen.

That five pounds Comfrey talked about would come in mighty useful, especially with this lean time coming on. If he could shoot the white goose it would not only be the money, there would be the sense of triumph. Manka was a challenge to his prowess as a hunter.

Down in his creek the "Twirp" was quite enjoying himself in spite of the cold and wet. If it had not been for the gull he would have gone up in our estimation (but never in Foxy's). He saw the gulls passing, he smelt the wind and the sea, he glimpsed the life on this bleak and drab coast, much hard work, much meanness, but always great skies like this, and a breadth of landscape that should have bred a breadth of vision. But he had not been impressed with the character of the country. No noble houses or fine parks, few trees and woods. Money, money, money, must be these people's God, the big farmers must indeed be rich. The labourers seemed poor and undersized. Inland it was not a pretty country, only the sea and the loneliness of the marshes made it bearable.

Suddenly he heard the geese. It was the first time he had ever heard that wild music which, to Foxy's ears, was so dearly familiar. People who hear that sound for the first time are sometimes struck dumb with astonishment, almost awe. There is no sound like it in the world.

Turning seawards he saw them coming off the banks, long lines of them and scattered bunches that hung, apparently stationary, like little clouds. And as he watched, he saw party after party going in over the bombing range and then a nearer skein close by. He crouched low and then a skein of seven came low for him over the marsh. In front was a big white bird. A swan, perhaps?

Against the wind the geese laboured slowly, swinging up and down at each fierce gust. At no time were they more than fifty feet high, an easy shot if they passed above him. He crouched yet lower with fast-beating heart. My word! Supposing he shot a goose his first time out! That would be something to boast about!

Nearer and nearer they came, their voices growing louder. He waited until he could hear the swish of their wings and then he rose on one knee. Right above him was Manka and Manka had not seen him. The other geese had, however, and with a cry of alarm they towered. The "Twirp" swung his gun and fired . . . and missed! He twisted round and at extreme range fired his second barrel at the white goose.

Foxy, away in Mudhorse creek, had seen the line of geese heading over the "Twirp" and when he saw Manka he groaned. He saw the figure rise from the gully and two jets spring from the muzzle of the gun, followed a second later by the sound of the double shots. What Foxy saw made him jump from the gully. The white goose was down!

Manka had never been aware of the gunner below him. This was strange in so experienced a bird, but birds, like humans, sometimes make mistakes, they grow careless and the spring was in his blood. At the sound of the first shot he jumped upwards and then something hit him on his right wing like a red-hot mallet. He staggered, desperately endeavouring to keep on an even keel, but the air no longer bore him, he fell, slanting, to the marsh. So strong was the wind it bore him backwards, over the man's head. Terrified, Manka saw the "Twirp" spring from the gully with his gun smoking in his hands, eyes dilated and mouth open.

In a moment Manka had run across the marsh and tumbled head first into a gully. The tide was still coming in and he kept close under the overhanging bank. He slipped in under a fringe of draggled sea-lavender and hid, neck straight out, as quiet and well concealed as a hiding moorhen.

The creek wound all ways and in a few moments, though the "Twirp" was certain he had marked Manka down, he soon completely lost his sense of bearing. He ran wildly across the marsh away from Manka, peering into the grips and scanning the marsh on all sides. Manka could hear the steps dying away and the heavy breathing growing less, and he lay where he was for he knew he was well concealed.

Across the marsh the "Twirp" saw Foxy running. He shouted and waved his arms. Foxy had a dog and the goose would soon be found. Foxy came up, panting. The "Twirp" was surprised at Foxy's excitement, it was decent of him to come and help like this, along the bank he had thought him a surly fellow.

"I've got a goose down! A dead bird, I'm sure!"

"Mister," said Foxy, "I've bin after that there white goose for years. You got 'im all right. Jess" (this to the dog) "come you here and seek. Seek, Jess!"

The dog bustled about the creeks, ears flapping as it sprang from tussock to tussock.

"It fell here somewhere," said the "Twirp" miserably, "it must be here!" And then, far down a drain, almost on the sand, they caught a glimpse of white. Both men ran, the dog with them. But when, after going a long way round to cross a dyke, they came up to it they found the body of the common gull.

"That isn't it!" shrieked the "Twirp," "it's a blasted gull. I tell you I shot a goose. We must find it! There's half a crown for you if you do!"

"Half a crown!" thought Foxy, "two quid, more like!"

But though they searched everywhere they could not find Manka. Once they passed within ten yards of where he was hiding, but the dog had got on the trail of a pheasant and was chasing it to the bank, heedless of the cracked roars of Foxy.

"Reckon that gull must 'ave been your goose, Mister," said Foxy, though he knew the goose was down.

He would come back when the "Twirp" had gone, and find him, even if he searched all day.

"We'll 'ave to be getting back to the bank," said Foxy, "the 'Old Man's' making" (indicating the tide).

Darkness had come, over the Wash the lights began to jig, the wind had died. All day Foxy had searched but found nothing and had gone miserably back to his cottage.

The "Twirp" was on his way back to London and was now speeding in his high-powered car at eighty miles an hour beyond Newmarket.

Round the big buoy the tide surged and gurgled, bobbing it up and down. Geese came clamouring back to the sea.

And far out on the sands was Manka, a crippled Manka with all his flight feathers of his right wing cut away, at the mercy of any prowling gunner that happened along the marshes. He would have to live, somehow, until his flights grew again. It would take weeks, most of the summer. His companions would be going back to Spitzbergen, he would have to stay. He did not of course realize this, a bird cannot reason like a human being. But he knew he was in great danger, that now he must skulk and hide, feeding on the marshes only at night.

Had Foxy guessed Manka was only winged he would have searched the marshes night and day to get him. But he thought he must be killed and that the body had gone out on the tide. The other geese on the sand-banks, sensing something was amiss, would not have Manka in their midst, they chased him away with out-stretched necks, hissing and beating their wings. Wild geese will not tolerate a wounded companion in the gaggles, sometimes they will even kill a wounded bird, obeying some strange instinct. Nature has no use for cripples, they are a danger and a hindrance.

So Manka went off by himself, a draggled and very unhappy Manka, listening to every gull's cry and dreading each succeeding dawn. He must use his wits now . . . if he was ever to see the Esker Bluffs again.

Chapter Six
WILLOWHILLS

And now came high spring, so full of hope and promise. The world grew green again, the sky a deeper blue. The April showers passed across the marshes, followed by the sun, the huge fields were patterned with red and gold and grey, the distant farms masked, for a moment, by veils of glistening rain.

IF Manka had been in danger when he had the use of his wings, he was in grave peril now. He was prey to roving foxes (though they were rare in this part of the country) and any gunner might shoot him like a rat.

He had come to depend on his powers of flight, but he had also grown accustomed to the loss of this power in the moulting season, for wild geese, like wild duck, moult out their flights every summer and for ten days or so they are helpless. This experience was to stand him in good stead.

He fed at night now, whatever the state of the moon. Loneliness and helplessness he felt, but not as we should feel them. With him his disability was an unwearying fear and gnawing discomfort. He feared every passing gull's shadow, every mallard springing from a dyke caused him to crouch low. During the hours of light he dare not go out to the sands where he would have been conspicuous. A wild goose is a large bird and can be seen a long way off, and a white goose shows up for an even greater distance.

Now came a great wind to comb the marshes, it played with the gulls and rooks, tossing them like leaves, it sent the white spray flying around the big buoy and blew curtains of dried sand whirling across the flats.

The rooks from Mellons Platt rookery loved these days, they flung themselves about and let the wind take them, wheeling

high like vultures round and round, mere specks in the upper
sky.

Mellons Platt was loud with the bleat of lambs and Billy was a
busy man; it was the busiest time of the whole year.

In one of the poplars along the sea-wall a pair of big mistle
thrushes ("horse thrushes" the country people call them) had a big
mossy nest in a forket, and the male bird mounted guard, chasing any
hoodie or carrion that came near.

Partridges no longer came on the marsh in coveys, all had
paired, and the pheasants kept to the land. Foxy, unable to shoot,
spent his time wandering about the marshes, sometimes giving Billy
a hand with the lambing when the latter required help. Billy was
his most valuable ally and it paid him to keep up the friendship.
This was lucky for the white goose; had Foxy been able to use his
gun then, Manka's story would have ended.

Foxy had set several snares by the marsh wall, and in the early
mornings he would wander along to see if he had caught anything.
He very often found a hare in the gateway snares, but rabbits were
scarce along the bank. Soon he would gather the samphire that
grew out on the distant muds; it made excellent pickle and he sold
many bundles in the season. It has a strange wry taste, pregnant
with the sea; some people consider it the best of all pickles. And
there was always the chance of rare migrants at this time of year
which he could sell to collectors. The shooting had to be done by
stealth, for if he were seen carrying a gun during the close season there
would be trouble. The sergeant was no friend of Foxy's; they had
met in the past and would meet in the future, always to Foxy's
disadvantage.

Foxy had shot many rare creatures; bitterns, night herons, avocets,
and ruffs; quite an imposing list, had he totted it up. But though he
spent many hours scanning the marshes with his glasses he never
saw Manka, or guessed the white goose was still alive.

And now came high spring, so full of hope and promise. The
world grew green again, the sky a deeper blue. April showers

passed across the marshes, followed by the sun; the huge fields were patterned with red and gold and grey, the distant farms masked momentarily by veils of glistening rain. Caw! Caw! Cowak! Cowak! called the rooks from Mellons Platt as they fed their husky-voiced squeakers. Hundreds of spring migrants filled the marshes; redstarts, black redstarts, warblers, whinchats and stonechats, cuckoos, chiffchaffs, swallows, and godwits.

The geese had gone and Manka had heard them go. In his agony he ran along the sands and flapped his useless wings, scattering the clouds of waders right and left.

But he could not rise, the earth held him down, bound and helpless. He swam out into the Wash, feeling the pull of the tide, but instinct told him it was folly to go too far from land, once out to sea he must perish. So he crawled back to the shore, feeling again the firm sand beneath his paddles.

He heard the wild music die away to the North and knew he must remain.

There was no moon on the night the geese went, but there were stars. There was no wind, only the movements of the tide, sucking about the big buoy. He knew by some strange instinct how the highroads of the sky were thronged with pilgrims, up there among the stars, countless unseen travellers, high in the night, the world at their command. There came to him the whisper of many wings, all manner of birds on passage, each with set purpose; whole armies of them, some departing across the sea, others coming in. Those same forces that moved the tide round the buoy, that set the winds blowing and the lambs bleating, urged them on their way. Little wings, big wings, rounded wings, pointed wings, quick beats, slow beats; all hurrying, hurrying with great purpose.

Poor Manka beat his wings in frenzy. He jumped, but returned again to the sand, pulled back by tremendous forces of which he had no conception. Never before had he sensed so strongly the pull of the earth's attraction.

Across the sky a shooting star fell, blazing a white trail to the dark rim of the horizon, snuffing out suddenly as a match is snuffed in water.

A tiny shadow passed over his head and fell exhausted in the sea-lavender. It was a chiffchaff, new from the dark forests of Lithuania. Other shadows fell, like moths, from the stars; willow warblers and redstarts, all settling to rest awhile before pushing on South.

The tiny wavelets creamed across the sands licking his paddles, and weary Manka slept with one eye half open. A spiny thing like a hedgehog gone wrong came bobbing past the sand-bar. The sea-urchin was dead, one with the empty razor shells and ropes of seaweed. The tide rolled it over and bore it on.

The dawn came and with it the sun, that shone so magically through the swaying daffodil carpets by Mellons Platt and made a glory of the coloured squares of bulb fields, where toiling women bent among nodding, painted cups of colour.

The apple blossom was coming out, and the blackthorn; gold-finches were busy among the snowy petals. Swallows twittered happily on the ridge of the great barn that had echoed to many a roaring harvest home. But it was yet cold in those flat lands, there was a sting in the wind, the winter grass showed in yellow tufts upon the pastures.

The curlews no longer came to Leader's Drove in large flocks, they had gone North to the hills to breed. In the dykes there was still a dead rustle of slender reeds, though new green rods were push-ing upwards among the dead. Big golden globes of king-cups dotted the little meres, and sedge warblers chattered in the dykeside thickets, a bubbling reedy song that almost smelt of water-lilies, dragon-flies, and quiet reaches of bream-haunted water.

Reflected in the flashes on the marsh the April skies seemed an unbelievable blue, like coloured windows set among the grey-green tones, and when a gust of chill wind came blustering, scores of sparkling diamonds scudded across the surface. And in another moment those same carpets of blue would be bruise-black with dark storm-clouds and the surface pricked with silver tents of rain.

Poor Manka was blind to all this beauty. The feed on the marsh was poor compared to the rich fare upon the inland fields, the marsh grass was coarser and less delicate than the Solway pastures, the fine herbage the barnacle geese love so much. His breastbone had lost its padding of well-fibred flesh and his undertail coverts were stained with the salting mud. The whole of his breast was smeared with mud as well, he was no longer the perfect snow-white bird that had come to those marshes in the autumn. His paddles were calloused with much walking.

Foxy had got some temporary work with Mr. Comfrey of Willowhills. There was little doing now with the lambing, and the extra shillings were vital to comfort. Together with four men from Maplode St. Mark's he was clearing out a dyke on the boundary of the farm.

It was a dirty job, the odour of the black slimy mud stank abominably, for the dyke had not been cleaned out for years. Clots of frog-spawn, wriggling eels, and old bulbous reed roots were tossed up on the bank, smothering the first fragrant violets.

Farther along the dyke was an old stone bridge, half hidden in blackthorn bushes, each branch as white as snow with blossom. In the blackthorn a thrush was singing. Close by, under the arch of the bridge, where the little polypody ferns grew, there was a nice new, sweet-smelling nest of dried hay lined with mud, and in the cup reposed two eggs as blue as the April sky, the blueness of the eggs accentuated by black splodges. That fat speckled thrush had something to sing about, for they were indeed eggs to be proud of, and the morning was lovely. A flicker of reflected light from the water was playing underneath the arch in waving lines of light.

The mother thrush was away on Leader's Drove, hunting for worms. Later, when the full complement of eggs was laid, she would be chained for two weary weeks incubating them.

The men worked until midday and then went down to the bridge to have their lunch, lumps of bread and slices of cold fat bacon, enormous "doorsteps" that were champed with much gusto.

Far up in the sky a lark was singing, the notes came trickling down like drops of clear spring water. "Terwee, terwee, terwee, terweechit, it, it, tit, chiree, chiree, twee, twee!" As the lark rose high the song became fainter.

Foxy shaded his eyes with a dirty hand that smelt of dyke water, and tried to see the bird. But the light was so strong it hurt his eyes.

At the moment he became aware of a figure in the distance coming along the bank. It was Billy. When the shepherd came up he stopped to pass the time of day with the men.

They talked of lambs, of the weather, the dirty business of cleaning drains. Then, just as Billy was going on down the bank, he stopped and half-turned round, shouting to Foxy.

"Reckon I saw th' ole white goose up be Mudhorse this mornin'."

Foxy did not reply for a moment.

"That you couldn't, Billy, I saw 'im shot wi' me own eyes eight weeks gone, musta bin a gull you saw."

"Gull be ——!" shouted Billy, "'twas the old goose or 'is brother. Walkin' along, 'e was, on the mud. I never saw 'im fly. Reckon 'e was never shot at all. Mebbe 'e was winged."

Billy passed on down the bank, whistling.

Foxy returned to his work with impatience. What Billy had told him was very likely right. Manka was alive after all and had only been pricked. Every summer there are pricked geese about the coastal marshes. The men began to chaff him unmercifully and made Foxy so angry that he flew into a temper. That amused them all the more and he got no peace for the rest of the afternoon.

The time seemed to drag unduly, but at last they finished for the day and Foxy shouldered his shovel and stumped back along the bank.

When he got back to his cottage he never stopped for a cup of tea, though it was ready for him in the little parlour.

He got his glasses, and whistling his dog went straight back along the bank.

On his left were signs of the day's hard work, the long ribbon of black slime lying on the grass, and to-morrow's task, the choked dyke beyond, reed-grown and full of old willow roots.

Clouds of plover were wheeling over the tide, and some broke and came past him with thin keenings. The sun was sinking, a faint rose-red ball that promised another fine spring day, the muds were shell-pink and violet. Swallows were ranged along the telegraph wires, and far out on the marshes, sheep, like maggots, were grazing.

There was a promise that evening of the sunny days the future had in store, all the glory of the summer, and dry, dusty roads that beckoned mysteriously. Foxy stood on the plank bridge looking towards the marshes. There came to his nostrils that indefinable scent of spring, of new growth on the marshes, the faint odour of sea-aster. By Mellons Platt a cow was lowing for her calf, and children were playing in the village streets.

He took out his glasses from his pocket and scanned the marsh. He saw nothing but the creeks, and a solemn star, burning like a lamp, over the Wash. The light was going fast and it would be useless to search for Manka now, he must wait until the morrow; they'd have to do without him in the dyke for a bit, and he blessed the fact he was his own master.

And just as he was going to turn away, his glasses picked up a white smudge, far out on the muds. It *was* Manka, sure enough! Calling his dog to heel, he got down below the level of a dyke bank and walked out towards the sea. He knew this creek well, it would take him to within fifty feet of where he had seen Manka, provided the goose did not move.

It was a big dyke with sloping sides of mud; luckily for Foxy the tide was out, but it was tiresome walking in the soft stuff and, where the numerous side gulleys ran in, the mud was deep and dangerous. From the shepherd's hut on the bank a dog began to bark, persistently; over the Wash the star grew brighter.

When Foxy had progressed a couple of hundred yards he took off his cap and raised his head, parting the wiry stems of sea-lavender to get a better view. There was Manka, not fifty yards away, cropping the grass. There was no doubt about it, Foxy could see the wing that was turned towards him was flightless.

Very soon the banks of the creek lowered as he got out more towards the sea. He must show himself now. He was on the seaward side of Manka, for the creek had wound about.

It looked as though Manka's number was up. At that moment a redshank, that had been feeding round a bend of the creek, rose shrieking in alarm and Foxy cursed under his breath. When he next peeped over, Manka was running away across the marsh. Man and dog scrambled up the bank and gave chase.

They saw Manka flop over the edge of a bank and vanish and when they came up there was no sign of him. Foxy urged the dog to "go seek" and it departed with splattering feet and flapping ears.

Foxy searched up creek and the dog went down.

The light was going fast, and for a moment Foxy thought that Manka might even yet give him the slip, perhaps it was true what men said, that the white goose was bewitched.

And then, all at once, Foxy found himself looking straight into Manka's beady eyes as he crouched, neck stretched out, under the overhanging lip of a bank.

For a moment the man was struck immobile. He could not believe his eyes. Already the dog was coming back and in the excitement Manka might be injured if the dog caught him, for he was hard-mouthed. Foxy gathered himself together and fell forward across the drain, pinning Manka to the mud. For a moment there was a brief struggle, in which Manka bit and flapped his wings. Then Foxy slipped his hand down and got Manka by the pink paddles and the next moment he was lifting him into the air out of the reach of the dancing spaniel.

Foxy really could not believe he held the white goose in his

Leader's Drove and Willowbills Farm

hands at last. Five pounds' worth of goose in good money! What a stroke of luck!

Manka's head was turning from side to side, almost like a snake. His beady eye was urgent with fear, and Foxy could feel the little heart beating like a sledge-hammer. He tucked the goose under his arm and triumphantly made his way back to the sea-wall.

Manka wriggled against the rough blue jersey, smearing it with mud from the drain, but he was held in a firm grip and every time he struggled Foxy squeezed him until all the breath left his body.

It was an elated Foxy that kicked open the cottage door and stood for a moment dazed by the bright oil lamp.

"Why, whatever 'ave you got there, Fred?" asked Mrs. Foxy.

"What's 'ee look like, mother?"

"Why! it's the white goose, ain't it?"

"Reckon so, I've got 'im at last. Didn't I tell you I would?"

Mrs. Foxy could only stare and say MY! several times.

"Somewhere, somehow," Foxy had said. . . . Well, his boast was no idle one. There would have to be some free pints now at the Black Swan, and they would have to eat grass, the lot of them. Foxy had never felt happier since he was a boy.

He took Manka out to the shed where he kept his rusty bicycle and cleared a place on the dirty floor with his foot.

He felt Manka's breastbone; the bird was thin, as thin as a rake, all skin and bone.

"Well, me beauty, you've led me a pretty dance, but I've got you now, you'll never trouble me no more. I'll take you up to Mr. Comfrey to-morrer. You'll be nice and comfy for the rest of your life; no worries, no gunners, no bother!"

He passed his hand along Manka's back almost lovingly. Then he caught him by the neck and pulled the goose's head close to him. "You'll never lead me a dance no more you ——!"

Manka darted out his head and caught Foxy's thumb by the

ball. He bit hard, and Foxy threw the goose to the floor with an oath. He slammed the door and locked it, and Manka, crouching in one corner, heard the man's steps dying away.

"Well," said Foxy, drawing up his chair to the table. "I'll take 'im round to Comfrey to-morrer and get that fiver 'e promised me. Reckon *that* old goose won't bother me no more!" But Foxy was wrong.

Left alone in the dark shed, Manka stood motionless. Only his head on the graceful white neck turned now and then as he listened. There was a pile of onion-skins on the floor under a bench, together with sacks of rotting potatoes that smelt badly. After a while, mice rustled in the skins. Manka was terrified at the tiny furtive sounds. Through the closed door came the piping of a redshank that was crossing the sea-wall. Manka looked at the dim cobweb-draped window and saw the stars in the velvet blue of the night sky. After a while the silence reassured him, and he began to walk, or rather stalk across the floor. One of the mice streaked out of the shadow of the bench, and Manka jumped aside with a squawk of alarm. But the mouse was more scared than Manka, it thought a great white owl was in the shed.

All through the night he heard the sounds of peewits and curlew on the marshes. Soon the moon rose, and made four squares of light that moved over the floor. Manka walked away, and hid under the bench in the corner. . . . As soon as it got light Foxy went to the shed, first looking in through the window. There was no sign of Manka, only nervous white splashes on the dirty floor where onion-skins were scattered. He went to the door and opened it a little way, poking his head in and looking round. He saw Manka in the corner, motionless, tail outwards. He threw down some chicken corn and left a pannikin of water. Then he went up to Willow-hills to see Mr. Comfrey. He found him feeding his geese in the pen.

"Well, Foxy, how are you getting on with the drain?"

"Nearly up to the bridge, Mr. Comfrey, but it ain't the drain I've come to see you about."

"No?"

"No. It's about that white goose you said you'd gie me a fiver for if I catched 'im. Does that offer still stand?"

"Yes, Foxy, course it stands, but the white goose was shot last February."

"Well, wot would you say if I told you I had 'im safe and sound in my shed?"

"I should say you were a liar, Foxy."

"Well, mebbee I am, but I've got 'im there sure enough, as large as life and not a scratch on 'im save his crippled wing; 'e was never killed at all as I thought, only winged, 'e's a pensioner an' bin on the marshes ever since."

Comfrey put the basket down carefully on the ground, and stared speechless.

"But you can't have him, Foxy, it can't be true!"

"True enough, Mr. Comfrey. Wot about coming down and 'aving a look at 'im?"

As they walked back down the lane Foxy told Comfrey the whole story, how Billy had seen the bird and how he had gone out at dusk and caught Manka by the creek.

Comfrey was so excited he could hardly speak; he would not believe Foxy until they had opened the door of the shed and Foxy had pulled Manka out by the paddles and held him up admiringly.

"My! What a beauty!" breathed Comfrey, "what a beauty!" He passed his hand along the smooth back and felt Manka's breastbone.

"Poor devil! he's thin, isn't he? can't have got much grub out there."

They took Manka up to the pen and here they made an examination of the injured wing. The joint was still slightly swollen, but no bone was broken, only five vital flight feathers were missing.

"'E won't fly for a bit, but you'll 'ave to pinion 'im afore the flights grow agin."

They put Manka down and watched him run to the other end of the pen and crouch against the wire. The other geese scattered and eyed the new-comer with alarm. "He'll be all right after a bit," said Comfrey.

He put his hand into his pocket and pulled out a bundle of notes. Into Foxy's dirty palm he counted five pound notes and the rabbit tooth showed in a smile. "Allus said I'd get 'im, Mr. Comfrey. Told Billy I would, and the fellers down at the Black Swan. Reckon I shall 'ave some free booze to-night."

Manka's life in the pen was perhaps better in some ways than the awful skulking existence on the marshes. He had plenty of nourishing food and after a week or two he ceased to sulk, head into corner, and fed with the waterfowl. But when the other geese were resting or bathing in the pond the white goose would be pacing the wire, up and down, up and down, in a ceaseless sentry-go.

For he could see the wide fields, the leaning willows, the far grey-green slope that was the sea-wall, the golden ricks and lichen-covered roofs of the farm. And sometimes a drift of birds rose above the bank as the wader flocks exercised in the sunlight. These flocks were not nearly so large as in winter, for most had gone away to breed. But always on the coast there were unmated birds or juvenile flocks, which stayed about the muds all summer.

Often Manka would turn his head sideways and watch the passing clouds, against which the tiny speck of a hovering kestrel was sometimes hung, and the blue spaces where once he climbed with such ease and freedom. He should have been away across the sea, listening to the sound of the fall, playing with other unmated geese on the marshes of Sassen Bay.

When Comfrey brought the geese their food, Manka stood apart and would never feed with them. Comfrey had to throw some grain down especially for him in one corner of the pen, and only after the man had gone back to the farm would Manka feed.

Then came the days of heat in that flat country of dyke and drain. In all that wide land there was no refuge from the sun, the cool shadows on the grass were a rarity. The bulbs had been harvested and earth fresh tilled, the long white roads shimmered and jumped in the unwearying heat and the geese thankfully sought shade under the twisted apple trees. All day long the goldfinches sang among the leaves where tiny green apples were forming, and the cutters were busy in the mowing grass. The sweet smell of the drying hay was wafted to Willowhills; Comfrey was working from dawn to dark, his face baked a leathery red by the summer sun.

On the marshes a great change had come about. The sea-lavender was in flower and so were all manner of marsh plants. In every dyke meadow-sweet showed its crumby white flowers, scenting the air. Each ditch held a sedge warbler and many mallard had young swimming with them through the reed forests in the level drains.

Day after day Manka watched the swallows chattering over the roof ridge. Sometimes they passed close over the pen and dipped into the little pond. Many came collecting mud at the margin of the water, the white-rumped eave-swallows with them, walking awkwardly with their absurd little feet as they gathered balls of mud in their bills.

Slowly the water in the pond receded, and the mud caked and flaked in hundreds of cracks. But even during the hottest weather this pond never quite dried up, and the geese were thankful for the water.

One day Comfrey, when he came to feed the geese, noticed that the flight feathers of Manka's wing were growing. The goose had put on flesh and looked in good condition; indeed the rest and good food had put a new strength into him, his plumage was now as white as ever. He chased Manka and caught him, making a thorough examination of the wing. The goose would have to be pinioned. He must come down one morning when he could spare a moment, and get Foxy to do the job.

A week later, when Comfrey was coming back across the plank bridge by the middle drain he slipped and broke his leg. He lay in agony for two hours, shouting and calling, but no one answered but the gulls. When at last he was found he was nearly unconscious with pain, for he had tried to crawl up the sloping bank. They took him straight off to hospital. Mrs. Comfrey looked after the geese.

Foxy heard of Comfrey's accident in the bar of the Black Swan.

"Well, Foxy, 'eard the news?" asked the landlord, drawing down the handle of the beer-engine until the white froth topped the glass.

"Gone and bruk 'is leg up be the middle drain. They say 'e musta slipped as 'e was crossin' over and 'e lay there a couple o' hours afore 'e was found. Bad go, wasn't it, specially just now, wi' harvest cummin' on an all."

Foxy made a noise that was meant to be sympathetic. Then he quickly drained his glass and stumped out of the bar. He went straight back to his cottage. Foxy had had another of his "ideas."

That morning the postman had come up to the cottage, where Foxy, in his shirt sleeves, leaning over the faded blue gate, awaited his arrival. Letters were rare at Foxy's cottage.

He took the envelope and without looking at it put it in his pocket and went round the house to the lean-to shed. Holding it up to the light of the dim little window he saw a London postmark. Foxy knew who it must be from. Professor Ritchie had corresponded with Foxy before. He was the greatest authority on wild geese in Britain, with the possible exception of Peter Scott. His collection of wildfowl at Englefield Park was unrivalled,

Ducklings among the reed forests

Foxy opened the envelope carefully and read slowly, as all labouring men do, spelling out the words aloud.

ENGLEFIELD PARK,
July 20

DEAR FORDHAM,

I hear, from roundabout channels, that an albino goose has been caught and that you effected his capture. If you still have it for disposal I should be glad to hear from you. If it is a genuine albino pinkfoot I can offer you twenty pounds for him. Perhaps you will let me know by return of post. I shall be at the above address until the middle of August.

Yours,
JAMES RITCHIE

Foxy re-read the letter several times and swore softly. Fancy parting with Manka to Comfrey for a paltry fiver! What a fool he had been. Twenty pounds. Phew! Foxy whistled.

The news of Comfrey's accident seemed like a dispensation of Providence to Foxy. It did not take him long to make up his mind. It would be a long time before Comfrey was out of hospital and Mrs. Comfrey was a simple woman. The whole thing was easy.

Hadn't Comfrey told Foxy himself that the white goose must be pinioned? Well, the chances were he hadn't been pinioned; Comfrey was a great one for "putting off things" and he never did like the job of pinioning his geese. Foxy had done most of his birds for him.

The whole plan was beautifully simple. He could say Manka had flown away.

The midsummer moon was large, rising over the quiet marshes and stooked fields. Tired poppy-heads drooped downwards, the ladies bedstraw in the ditches shone whitely. Moonlight made a pattern from the dykeside reeds; not a breath of wind was stirring them.

Hours back the carts had left the fields, laden with sheaves, their rut-marks and fallen wisps were on the stubble. Mallard quacked in the dykes. Up the long level path of light that was the drain, a mallard duck swam with her babies, a late brood. They broke the moon's reflection into a hundred pieces as they clove a furl of water up the centre of the dyke.

Maplode church struck one o'clock; there was a sense of brooding peace, of summer's end.

Foxy came across the cornfield, keeping to the shadow of the stooks. The cut poppies were no longer red, they looked brown in the moonlight. He stole through the orchard where also shadows were patterned. Under the trees it was quite dark. He opened the door of the pen and slipped inside, standing quite motionless.

Many of the geese were down by the pond, a few were resting on the rim of mud above. And on the far side of the pen, under one of the apple trees, was Manka, standing very straight and watchful. He had seen Foxy (I was going to say his old enemy, but Manka did not know Foxy was his enemy, he regarded all men alike, with fear and distrust) and he let out a honk of alarm.

Foxy had a sack over his arm and he moved forwards very stealthily from bole to bole of the apple trees. Manka began to walk quickly away towards the open part of the pen.

This wouldn't do at all, Foxy must corner him before he got to the other geese and disturbed them. He ran out of the shadow and made a rush at Manka.

Manka let out a squawk and spread his wings. He ran with great rapidity between the trees and dashed out into the open. The white wings threshed violently, and with quite a sickening horror Foxy saw the white goose rising into the air.

Woof! woof! woof! He cleared the wire and went right over the ridge of the barn.

The other geese scattered in alarm and set up a great cackling that awoke the Comfrey's cur by the barrel in the yard.

In a moment the quiet night was hideous with sound, and Foxy made away as fast as he could across the cornfield to the bank. Perhaps Manka was down in the field, he had flown with a very unsteady flight. But he scanned the stubble in vain. Behind him the dog was still barking and a light had appeared at an upper window.

He heard Mrs. Comfrey shouting to the dog, and the geese in the pen were still cackling.

When Foxy reached the sea-wall he stood a long time looking out over the marshes. They were sweetly peaceful under the moon, plovers were calling far out on the tide's edge, and a big white owl came beating up the bank.

There was no sign of Manka.

Foxy swore. He'd made a fair mess of things now. He could now say, with truth, that Manka had indeed "flown away."

Chapter Seven
FREE

This world was his again to roam where he willed; by starlight and sunlight, to far lands, to remote hill lochans, Solway, Cromarty, Tay and Spitzbergen, might know him again.

FREE!

Manka's wings bore him away, unsteadily it is true, but they held the air long enough for him to cross the sea-wall and the breadth of the marsh. The tide was running out, he pitched in the main drain, and the current bore him beyond the bell buoy. Friendly tide, it had been waiting to receive him, and now it took him across the flats with a gentle motion. No more two-legged creatures jabbering and staring at him, no more pacings behind the wire, no more wistful gazing at the sky. Foxy had been the indirect means of his escape. Even Manka would not have guessed his wings could bear him up, the sudden fright had saved him.

This world was his again to roam where he willed; by starlight and sunlight, to far lands, to remote hill lochans, the Solway, Cromarty, Tay and Spitzbergen might know him again. Had Comfrey not slipped when crossing the bridge, Manka's life would have been very different, he would have been pinioned and chained to the earth for the rest of his life. The loss of the power of flight is as dreadful to a wild bird as loss of sight to a man.

Manka would never be caught again.

Dawn was coming, the dawn of a new era for Manka, it came slowly from over the rim of the sea, a misty dawn that promised a hot day.

Here was the sandbank where he had always come, though not a goose had rested there since early spring. Crabs lay about, razor shells, and the droppings of sheld-duck. But he did not stay, he rose again from the water and flew northwards along the edge of the tide, skimming low until he was lost in the misty distance where the far finger of Boston Stump pointed to the dawn sky.

Summer was nearly done, the hedges were showing spots of rust, the stubbles cleared. Clinging to hawthorns bordering the lanes were wisps of straw that told of passing wagons piled high with harvest, fruit of the glorious sun. The telegraph wires along the sea-wall were thronged with swallows and martins. In the dykes the green reed jungles were turning yellow and rotting down; it was a time of misty mornings and glorious sunsets. The colourful skies were reflected on the muds and strings of mallard passed over the marshes night and morning, bound for the stubbles inland.

At evening time the pop of guns was heard once more, and many young mallard fell; others were spared by fickle chance to benefit by experience and live. The curlews were back on the tide, the godwits had gone, the marshes were alive with teal, indeed it seemed the commonest duck. They loved the sea-aster and fed upon it, later they would move away.

Manka had left the Wash and was exploring new country round the Humber. By this time he could fly well, and every night he flighted out to the upland stubbles across the high wolds. Many a farmer saw him passing, and wondered what manner of fowl he was, so white and large. It was full early for the geese, and the lonely stubbles were empty, save for hares and lapwings, the latter in thousands. These feeding-grounds entailed long flights to and from the Humber, but Manka found peace there, and plenty. Night after night he flighted from Sunk Island, passing, far below, the shining sickle of the Trent. Lonely were those nights on high uplands with only twittering larks and loping hares for company.

Partridges were numerous, crouching like scattered clods on the dun-coloured stubbles.

He listened eagerly for the sound of returning geese but he heard only the sigh of the wind among the twisted thorns and the boom of ships' sirens on the Humber.

To another world belonged the farmyard smells, the wire pen, the the ceaseless walking to and fro, the sinister figure of Foxy slinking under the moonlit apple trees. Manka now dreaded human beings more than ever and even the far glimpse of a man on some distant pasture would make him spread his great wings and take to the sky. Every day he could fly with greater ease, at no time since his early days had he been in better condition. He was now fully grown, and weighed five and a half pounds, which was a good weight for his age. His flight feathers were developed, there was no suggestion that his wing had ever been scarred by shot.

How the smoke lay on the land those September evenings! Every hamlet had its reek of smoke, sweet smelling and blue. In the autumn, the spirit that is England seems distilled about the woods and fields, and even the great cities take on a new romance, fragrant and rare.

Time and again Manka listened, eager for the sound that had been silent for so long. And then came a night when he was rest-less and watchful. He constantly stopped feeding, turning his head. In the farmyards the tame geese and ducks were restless too, gabbling together and cocking boot-button eyes skywards, for in them arose a half-forgotten memory that filled them with gnawing disquiet. Up there the wild geese were passing across the stars, bound again for the land they loved, drawn by a longing as old as the world. A faint chorus fell from the blue vault whither the useless wings of the captives had long since ceased to climb.

And Manka, feeding near Eastoft on the Yorkshire Wolds, heard those voices and was glad. All the way from Spitzbergen and Ice-land had they come, back to this friendly little island that was so reposeful under the harvest moon. And, perhaps, in that ghostly music that grew nearer every moment Manka heard again the voice of the Esker river, and saw the snow-clad peaks and glaciers of his beloved Sassen Bay.

Though the geese passed over, Manka could not see them; the wild bayings seemed to be coming down from a vast height and after a while they died away towards the Humber.

Manka rose from the field and flew back to Sunk Island. There he found thirty-three tired Icelandic pinks all fast asleep. They heeded him not when he landed amongst them.

When, at dawn, they awoke and flew over the wolds, Manka went with them. Manka had come back to the old life, feeding with the gaggles and flighting out every day to the wolds. It was strange that in this particular gaggle which Manka had joined, there was not one goose from Spitzbergen. Possibly the Spitzbergen birds had gone straight to the Wash.

But Manka had no mate to look for or to cherish, he was still a bachelor. Wild geese do not mate until they are three years old or more. And then they mate for life.

The great autumn gales swept those high pastures by the Humber, sending the last leaves flying, and early came the snow, capping the high hills with white, mantling the ricks and farms and driving the fowl away.

The geese do not frequent the Yorkshire Wolds after December, there is no gleaning to be had on the stubbles.

Manka and the rest of the skein went up the coast until they came to Bamburgh, where a loneliness broods along the sands and there is a haunting romance that even the coming of the car and the aeroplane has not quite destroyed.

Fenham slakes used to be one of the finest fowling-grounds (for puntsmen) in Britain. That large flat expanse of glutinous mud that is covered only at the tides forms a wonderful feeding-place for wild-fowl of all kinds. The "zos" grass grows plentifully and on this the brent-geese and widgeon feed. The latter never haunt the slakes during the hours of light, but soon after dark they come in, great whispering companies, from the open sea. They pass high between the beacons and Holy Island and at dawn go out the same way. The brent, the black geese with a white neckband, feed during the day and very rarely do they fly inland. They are essentially sea-geese like the barnacle, and will not haunt stubbles or the arable fields.

Fenham slakes is also one of the ports of call of migrating wild-fowl. Why this is so, has never been quite understood. In this respect it resembles Scolt Head in Norfolk, but has not the variety of species one finds at the latter place.

Manka came to know the brent-geese well. They seemed more like ducks than geese, with their short tubby bodies and white undertail coverts.

Every morning at about ten o'clock (when the tides were right) the brents came in high over the castle, hanging like compact smuts against the grey autumn sky. Later, after Christmas, their numbers would be trebled. While Manka haunted the slakes there was only a small party of about fifteen brents using the bay.

Sometimes when the grey geese, Manka amongst them, were resting on the slake, a sinister shape would come sidling out from Holy Island. Manka, having several times had narrow escapes from punt guns, would croak an alarm, and take the skein over the sand-dunes to the Ross links. The grey geese did not feed very often on the slakes, they only resorted there for rest.

When the easterly gales blew, the gunners, hidden among the dunes at the point of the beacons (the horn of sand that forms one of the entrances to the slake) had great sport, for the wigeon and geese flew low. Given the right tide and the right wind it was a splendid place for the shoulder gunner.

Manka and the rest of the skein found good food in the remote fields behind the links. There was one particular field, not very far from the white farmhouse, that the geese loved above all others. Like Inchgarvie, and the other meadows by the Tay, the geese came every year, using the same pasture with unfailing regularity.

Nearer the dunes were little pools, rush grown, that held sweet water and the geese flighted there to drink. Teal, mallard and (at night) wigeon, haunted these little freshets, and as they were seldom shot it was a favourite sanctuary.

So good was the feed on those green, low-lying fields, and so rarely were they disturbed, that the geese stayed about the links until mid-January. At night they rested either on Fenham slakes or on the sands of Budle Bay on the Bamburgh side. They saw the lights of Holy Island shining across the muds and the distant refuge towers standing half-way over, between the island and the mainland. They heard the eternal boom of the surf on the long white sands. The spray hung in a faint haze, all along the line of the breakers between Holy Island and Bamburgh, with its misty castle that frowned upon the sea.

Rarely did the geese fly inland to the Cheviots, these were days of little work and much good fare, and the geese became perhaps a little lazy, and Manka a trifle more unwary.

One bright sunny morning, after resting out in Budle Bay, they came in to their favourite field. There had been a sharp frost over-night and the grass was crisp and glistening with silver; in the miry gateways the mud was iron hard, the puddles roofed with white ice.

As Manka came over the sand-hills he was surprised to see six geese already on the meadow. They were standing facing the wind with lifted heads. Where geese are, man is not, so Manka set his wings and glided in. Not until he was a few feet above the geese did he sense something was wrong. Those on the ground remained strangely immovable and never cackled a welcome or twisted their heads.

And as Manka, suspicious, turned into the wind, he saw a man crouching in a ditch that ran along the side of the field, not forty yards from the dummy geese. A honk of alarm and the whole skein rose. A second later Manka heard the dreaded crash of a gun and lead came whistling amongst the skein. One goose, close beside Manka, staggered, righted itself, staggered again, and then fell forward with outspread wings right on to Manka's back. The weight bore him downwards but he flew on, and a second later his "old man of the sea" rolled off and fell lifeless to the grass below.

That gunner had a tale to tell when he reached home, how the white goose had striven to save his companion's life. Few would believe him.

Thereafter the geese fed farther down the coast, though they still remained in the district. It was not long before every one who had a gun (and could get permission to shoot upon the fields) was out after the white goose. Luck was with him still, however, and not a man got a chance.

Sometimes in the quiet moonlight nights the geese could hear the dull murmur of the breakers coming from over the dunes. Day and night that sound was always there, more pronounced than the voice of the sea around the Wash. Those were the same sounds that St. Cuthbert must have heard on his little island, many and many a night. By the sea it is easy to understand Eternity. Time is not. Ceaseless movement, even on the calmest summer day; the rivers run for ever to the sea.

Then came the incident that drove the geese away from Ross for the rest of the winter.

Cattle were in the fields, mostly black Angus, and a few horses. Now Manka had come to regard these four-footed beasts as perfectly harmless, and frequently fed in the same field with them. One day when the geese were grazing in a small meadow behind the dunes a horse walked through a distant gateway and began to graze towards them. Manka, ever on the watch, was not suspicious, even when strange muffled sounds seemed to come from the horse's belly. And then Manka noticed the feet were rather strange, that the animal did not move with quite the same gait as an ordinary horse. A minute or two later something dropped out from between the horse's legs and fell on the grass. This again was not an unusual thing but the "something" was long, clubbed at one end. It was a gun. Inside the horse (which was in reality merely a horse's skin stretched on a wooden framework) were two men. Manka took wing.

The horse collapsed and in its place were the gunners. Their shots went wide, for the geese were out of range, but Manka was so badly shaken that he took the skein away North to his old familiar grounds about the Tay.

Rob, coming home one night from shooting wood-pigeons by Errol Park, heard the geese, and saw Manka flying at the head of a long string, just above the surface of the river, and he recognized his old friend. Next evening he went to the long stone breakwater that stretched out through the tall reeds to the water's edge. He walked along it with care, for there had been a sharp frost overnight, and the stones were slippery; with his rubber boots it was tricky going. At the end of the breakwater (built many years before in an effort to reclaim the marsh) there was a hollow in the stones which provided excellent shelter for a gunner. Occasionally Rob shot a goose from this side, but it was a dangerous place, both for dog and man, especially when the river was frozen.

At high water, large ice-floes were piled against the breakwater, and a bird falling among them was difficult to retrieve.

On either hand the tall reeds rose in a perfect forest; not a breeze swayed them, they formed a slender screen, black against the red in the West.

Out in the river some greylags were calling hoarsely, and as dusk fell Rob heard some more geese coming in from the hills. He did not expect a shot, for the Tay, unlike the Wash, is more a punter's ground than a shoulder gunner's, but occasionally the geese offered a chance, especially at the beginning of the season. As the moon rose, its pallid reflection rocked on the tide close to the stones of the breakwater. Each lapping ripple broke the disc of light, which flew together again.

Soon a long skein of pinks came along the edge of the reeds, Rob saw they were coming straight for the breakwater. He curled up in the bottom of the hide and the skein came right overhead. His heart gave a bump when he saw Manka, grey against the evening sky.

"Followed the old road in the old way"

Rob was a crack shot but fortune favoured Manka once more for as Rob fired, his foot slipped on the stones, and the shot that was meant for Manka hit his next astern. The stricken goose slumped down, falling with a crash among the floating ice-floes.

Manka and his companions stayed in the vicinity of the Tay until the end of the winter, and though he had many other escapes, he came safely through. The middle of April saw the skeins massing for their flight across the sea.

There was a new disquiet within Manka, apart from the pain that would not be denied; he longed for a mate. Already he had cast lustful eyes on many of the trim grey virgins among the skeins, but the sexual fever was not yet at its height and the choosing of a mate would take place among the glaciers of his native land.

By the end of April all the geese were moving off North. With them went Manka, filled with an unutterable longing to see the Esker bluffs once more.

They followed the old road in the old way, and the wild baying died across the hills. Rob, smoking by his fire and pulling the ears of his spaniel, heard them go over. He remembered Manka and wished him *bon voyage*. There would be no more goose voices on the river now until his blossom-laden apple trees were bare and black again.

Chapter Eight
GREY MANTLE

The winter was still upon this land. Advent and Sassen Bays were frozen solid, though the ice was beginning to show signs of breaking up. There were wheezings and crashings when the sun was at its height, large lumps of ice calved off the overhanging rock faces to slur and slush into the water. The high snow was melting, too, and streams and rivers became unbound again, turbulent with sound.

ON the second of May the first skein of geese came over Brent Pass and circled Sassen Bay. They landed on the marshes at the mouth of the Sassendal, but there was no white goose amongst them. Late in the afternoon of the sixth (if there can can be such a thing as "afternoon" in the Arctic) a white spot, together with sixty companions, came holding high over the bay. They wheeled, bugling, and the geese on the marshes answered. Manka was back home again, Manka as yet mateless, three pounds heavier than when he last heard the drum of the waterfall.

Winter lay still upon this land. Advent and Sassen Bay were frozen solid, though the ice was beginning to show signs of breaking up. There were wheezings and crashings when the sun was at its height, large lumps of ice calved off the overhanging rock-faces, to slur and slush into the water. The high snow was melting too, and streams and rivers, unbound again, became turbulent with sound.

Soon after their arrival the geese began to pair up, and great fights were witnessed on the Esker bluffs. The old ganders fought savagely, biting like dogs and buffeting each other with their wings. Poor Manka found no favour in the eyes of the eligible geese. Though he was tolerated in the skeins and allowed leadership (maybe his white form was easier to follow), when it came to the delicate business of choosing a mate, Manka was regarded as an oddity.

Anything out of the normal is looked upon with distrust by Nature and the geese were following their right instincts.

As wild geese do not breed until they are three years old, Manka had not experienced the pain of sexual desire. Apart from the colour of his plumage, he was in every other respect perfectly normal and healthy. He made advances to several likely looking ladies, but they turned him down, even though he savagely fought the other ganders who were also paying court. The ganders on the ledges chased him and would not allow him near the bluffs. Not one bird, but many, would band together and pursue him. It may have been that, though they knew he was a goose like themselves, his white plumage roused in their minds past experiences with big falcons and skua gulls.

Unhappy, he took long flights by himself, filled with a great hunger. He explored many lonely bays where geese seldom visited, he grew thin and out of condition. And then one day, flying close to the ruined hut on Starvation Point, he came upon an exhausted pink-footed goose. She sat among the stones with intucked bill, fast asleep.

Manka circled round, calling excitedly, but beyond pulling her head out from her scapulars she took no heed of him. He pitched on the foreshore and sat on a drift of old snow that half-covered the coffin. A few bones still remained, but the skull had gone; a wandering bear had carried it away as a plaything for her cubs.

Manka watched the little goose for some time and then began to walk towards her. When a few feet away he called, but she ignored him and continued to sleep. It had been a long and painful journey for her, a stray shot fired by a gunner on the Cromarty Firth had bruised her wing-joint and it had been long healing.

Manka walked all round her and sat down within a few yards. Finding his advances remained unnoticed he began to pace up and down, like a gander on sentry-duty by the nest.

All about, the saxifrage was coming into flower, millions of tiny pink buds covered the grey-green cushions, a brighter red in bud than later on. Here and there a flower had opened wide its petals, the poppies were also nodding their hairy pursed heads. It would not be long before they were in flower also. A soft wind blew over the marshes, and the sound of quarrelling gulls came from seawards where seals were disporting themselves among the ice-floes. Manka sat a long while with an air of proprietorship, and after a while he moved a little nearer to Grey Mantle and touched her gently with his bill. The goose withdrew her head instantly and dived at him, causing Manka to shuffle away a few paces, where he again sat down regarding her. After a while Manka began to feel hungry, so he walked away to the edge of the water and began plucking at grass blades. But he never went far from her. Two terns came and mobbed him, stooping and shrieking, for they had a little scrape in the shingle not far away where they would soon have eggs. Manka plucked half-heartedly at the grass, stopping every moment to take a look at Grey Mantle, who still slept soundly.

There was a blue mist rising over the bay; far away, bright against the blue sky, a line of peaks showed up vividly, bathed in sunlight. Always the sun appeared to be shining on that distant range, even when the country round Sassen was wrapt in cloud shadow; it seemed a promised land.

Not far away Manka heard the tinkle of a little stream. Higher up it flowed over a glacier, deep and swift, pent up between green walls floored with ice. As it felt its way between the hyperite rocks and mosses it became broad and shallow, split up into innumerable rillets.

Higher up among the hills a great mass of snow, falling with a muffled boom, suspended in the air a mist of snow crystals. The sun, shining upon these, made a pattern of tiny rainbows, most magical and rare. Sometimes there came the shattering roar of stone avalanches from the mountain-sides as hundreds of tons of debris came hurtling to the bogs below. These bogs were a mush of snow, stones, and mud, into which a reindeer would have sunk to the neck. Just off-shore, there was a family of little auks, diving and swimming in unison as though at drill. At a signal all dived together, reappearing at the same time, swimming left and then right, with a clockwork precision that a guardsman would have envied. The tide was high, and the sea lapped the stones twenty yards from the sleeping Grey Mantle. It jangled and bumped the blocks of ice that had calved off icebergs out in the bay. The sunlight on the far peaks began flooding down the mountain-sides towards the marshes, speeding across the snow-slopes and lighting up the emerald green of the moss-bogs. It came racing towards Starvation Point until even that forbidding spot, with its desolate hut and mouldering bones, seemed a place of warmth and beauty. It cast a strong blue shadow on the snow-patch behind the hut.

Among the boulders beyond the sleeping goose was a small patch, or spot, of white. Manka, idly watching it and feeling drowsy in the sun, was startled to see it begin to move.

Now snow-patches *do* move sometimes, especially when the sun shines. But this was on level ground among rocks. Manka's head went up, his neck very straight, and soon he stood up almost on tiptoe and gave a low "crank" of alarm.

Then he stalked slowly forward to investigate, turning his head from side to side to get a better view.

Down between the rocks a fox crouched low with flexed ears, the tip of his brush twitching slightly. Thirty yards away he saw the sleeping Grey Mantle, and beyond was Manka, very white in the sunshine, stalking slowly towards him.

The fox lay quite still, hoping the white goose would come within springing distance, but Manka was too wary. He *almost* recognized the fox for what he was, but was still not quite sure.

Grey Mantle withdrew her head at the low croakings of Manka, she recognized the danger signals and her little eye scanned her surroundings very closely. The fox was hidden from her by a large boulder, all she could see was the tumbled foreshore, twinkling ice-floes, the blue peaks across the bay. She became uneasy and at last rose stiffly, stretching her wing fanwise over her paddle. At that moment the fox sprang. He came like a charging tiger with brush uplifted.

But he was too late, both geese were in the air and passed low over his grinning mask and dripping ivories. He sat up and watched them go out over the sea where the auks were tumbling and diving, and he curled his brush round him quietly like a cat. Then he flexed back his ears and yawned, falling flat on his side to warm his belly in the sun. He gloried in the luxurious new warmth, and soon he rolled right over on his back with legs apart, the picture of utter abandon.

Two dots wheeled away beyond Starvation Point, one dot was grey, the other white. They settled close to the foot of a glacier whose great icy snout towered about them with caverns and caves of green glass filled with shadow.

All about were mighty ice-blocks, some the size of boulders, others as big as pantechnicons. The air was full of water voices, for the warmth of the sun was melting the higher ice-fields, and tons of water were draining away through the snow-bogs. All round was the spring song of Spitzbergen, the babble of waters, the call of the geese, and the crash of avalanches.

Manka walked round and round the little goose, "displaying," puffing out his white feathers and fanning his tail, but she ignored him. Instead of watching she began to preen, just as though Manka had not been there. How could she understand Manka had saved her life? How could he understand he had saved it?

For Manka the pain of loneliness was forgotten; the pain of possession had taken its place.

The minutes passed away. To the north the sun slid behind the icy peaks of Baldhead mountain and the unbelievable blue of the Colerado range became more intense. A snow-bunting was singing from a boulder and another answered. They joined combat in the air, for they were cock birds; tiny feathers flew. These birds were the commonest land bird on Spitzbergen. All day long, in summer, their sweet wild song comes from the stony hill-sides. Up among the boulders a hen snow bunting watched the warring males, affecting not to notice, in the same way Grey Mantle affected to ignore Manka, with feminine guile, which spurs on the male and whets his appetite.

The tide was dropping now, and a double line of skuas and gulls were lining up on the edge of the water, terns hovered and settled delicately again on the sea, the air was full of their raspy music.

Manka felt a great content, his pain was eased. The next day or two Manka waited on Grey Mantle. When she flew about the marshes Manka went with her, they kept away from the waterfall. A big gander from the bluffs spied Grey Mantle one morning, feeding among the mosses with Manka not thirty yards away. When the latter saw the strange goose, sweeping down and alighting on the moss, he went over and joined battle.

Wild geese can inflict quite a severe blow with their wings and soon the two ganders were fighting tooth and nail. White feathers flew, as well as grey, they worried at each other like terriers.

Soon the birds were sitting back exhausted among the emerald moss, gasping for breath with half-open bills. Grey Mantle was also sitting not far away, comfortably plucking the greenery about her, nibbling the saxifrage buds, and preening.

Manka rushed at his enemy again and managed to get on his back, biting the back of the gander's neck with his strong mandibles. The marshes rang with hoarse cackles of pain, until the discomfited gander broke free and flew low across the sunlit moss. Manka gave pursuit and brought his adversary down again near a little pool. But the grey gander was beaten, he escaped again and fled towards the bluffs, and Manka returned to Grey Mantle. For the first time she welcomed him, and the white gander, still full of the dominating spirit and a sense of conquest, took Grey Mantle for his mate, whether she would or no.

For their honeymoon they explored the coast northwards to Wijde Bay, and from thence through the Hinjlope Straits to

Barents Island. They found other geese nesting in the cliff-ledges of the East Coast, the little pied magpie geese that were familiar on the Solway. Like the pinks, they built high on the rock-face in inaccessible eyries; how their babies ever reached the talus below was something of a mystery, for from some of the nesting-sites sheer precipices fell away for hundreds of feet.

The waterfall ledges called Manka and Grey Mantle, and they went back in the first week in June. The nesting geese would have none of them, so after many battles, the white gander and his mate went away to Starvation Point. A little farther along the point a stream ran into the sea. Grass grew in patches, fine green grass, and on one side, the brook was sheltered by a mighty cornice of ice, hanging against the face of the rocks. Close by was a most curious ice-formation, a rounded lump of solid ice the size and shape of a haycock. In the top was a pool of water, of crystal clearness, about three feet deep. Snow buntings sipped the icy nectar, and sometimes foxes quenched their thirst there. Principally it was used as a bathing-place by buntings and phalaropes, for at one end the fairy pool was shallow, and when the sun shone the water became quite warm, which the sea never was.

Beyond it, like an enormous boot, was the snout of a great glacier which wound away up the valley among the mountains, in a wide path of knobbly ice. It was a lonely place, for there were no other geese in the vicinity, and Manka and Grey Mantle had for their only companions a pair of purple sandpipers who had a nest between a cleft of rock, half hidden by clumps of saxifrage. They resented the intrusion of the geese, and repeatedly mobbed them, partly because Manka was white and they confused him with a glaucous gull.

About fifty yards from the shore the stream split up round an island, a tiny boggy place of moss and grass, about ten yards across. When the stream was in full flood there was only a small area left and even that was soggy. Grey Mantle seemed to take a fancy to this place, for she felt protection from the water which ran on either side.

Every day they were there despite the constant nagging of the purple sandpipers. Grey Mantle began to make a scrape among the saxifrage cushions. She hollowed out a place by scratching with her paddles, and plucking the roots away with her bill, while Manka looked on admiringly. By the third week in June the first egg was laid, rather like a very large wild duck's egg. The goose and gander dare not leave it for long, even though it was carefully covered in the soft down from Grey Mantle's breast. By the first of July the goose was sitting on four eggs.

Manka stood guard and would allow no other bird anywhere near, and the purple sandpipers kept away and no longer worried them.

Very soon there was a trampled sodden path encircling the nest, where Manka had ceaselessly walked round and round. With three days of warm weather the river rose. Every day it ran louder and higher until it was rushing past the nest; Grey Mantle could almost dip her bill into the torrent as she brooded. Soon it was flooding over Manka's path till the saxifrage clumps were submerged, and the black mosses were bubbly, oozing beads of water at every step of a pink paddle.

It was an unusually warm summer for Spitzbergen and every day the crash of ice became more frequent. The geese became so used to the roar and rumble of these avalanches they ceased to trouble about them. When the eggs had been brooded for two weeks, the great overhanging cornice of ice suddenly came away from the rock-face and fell with an appalling noise right into the path of the stream. Its course was diverted and the island became almost high and dry. Still Grey Mantle sat her eggs with grave patience, for she felt stirrings within the thick shells.

Midges danced in the soft airs and the days and nights were like an English spring. Sometimes Manka took short flights over the snow-fields to exercise his wings, but he was always within sight of the island and his patient little wife.

And then one midnight, when the mists lay as white as milk

over the bay and everything was deathly still, a fox came stealing past the glacier foot and crouched behind a block of green ice, sniffing the air. Grey Mantle was sleeping on her nest, and Manka was likewise drowsing on the edge of the island, his paddles in the water.

The purple sandpipers saw the fox first, they came shrilling and planing about the glacier snout, bills held wide as they uttered their alarm notes. Grey Mantle and Manka awoke at once, and the former saw the fox, crouching not twenty yards away among the ice-blocks.

Just above it the mother sandpiper was scolding, standing on a ledge of ice while her mate circled round, mobbing the crouching ball of fur. Manka rose and joined the sandpipers. He circled, sounding the alarm, beating his big white wings and twisting his long neck sideways.

The fox crouched and snarled, once he sprang upwards in an endeavour to catch the swooping goose.

He had had many an egg from the island in the past, for Grey Mantle had not been the first goose unwise enough to choose the place for a nesting-site. Heedless of the mobbing birds the fox slunk down to the stream and crossed it at the shallowest point. Grey Mantle saw him coming and joined her mate, they flew round in circles crying piteously. But the fox was intent on getting to the nest. He soon found it, and ate the eggs at leisure. Weeks of toilsome patience had been in vain.

Having finished his meal, the fox trotted back across the stream, and when Grey Mantle and Manka alighted at once near the nest they found only scattered yolk, red with blood (for the eggs had been hard set) and a few scraps of shell. The down had been scratched out amongst the herbage and black moss. Grey Mantle sat down, miserably in the hollow and tried to imagine the eggs were still there for she was yet broody.

But next day they went away to the Sassendal, and joined the barren gaggles that were always there in the summer-time.

As the brief summer sped, Manka and Grey Mantle began to lose their flight feathers. Soon they were as helpless as wingless beetles.

Away on the Esker bluffs, Manka's parents had hatched off another lusty brood, they were now in the bogs, where Manka had been taken long ago. The other geese were likewise dribbling away from the bluffs, and when Manka took Grey Mantle up the river one morning, he found only two remaining pairs on the ledges. But it was too late now to contemplate another brood for the summer was drawing to an end.

He visited his old breeding-ledge, fouled by the last family. Many thousands of miles had his wings borne him since he was last upon that rock, many adventures had been his; he had lived a dozen dull men's lives in the free winds of heaven. The reindeer's horn had gone, but a snow bunting was perched on the stones opposite, jingling his little song that cut through the drum of the fall.

Very occasionally the geese saw ships standing off the bay, threading their way through the ice-floes, but no anchor was dropped, they all passed by the uninviting solitudes of Sassen Bay.

So the wild grey geese were left alone to enjoy this, their kingdom, peopled by hovering terns, and sleek seals rolling among the floes. Gales came at the latter end of August, gales that set the ice a-clash, that boomed in dull thunder among the wild passes of the mountains. Spitzbergen is one of the most lonely and desolate places on the earth, its haunting power is remembered by those who have visited the island; truly a fitting birthplace for the wildest of wild birds.

Grey Mantle had forgotten her sorrow, for sorrow to a bird (even of a goose's intelligence) is short-lived. She was happy with her mate in this lonely land. By the end of August their "flights" had grown again, and once more they could make excursions across the island, always returning to the bay at night.

There were no guns to fear when on these happy wanderings.

Mists, stealing in from the sea, filmed the mountains with a lovely blue glaze during those happy, peaceful days. Manka and Grey Mantle had no family cares, they were free to get the most out of life and they were happy and content. Sometimes snow squalls came and briefly whitened the rocks on the lower slopes, gusts of cold rain sheeted the hills, varying days of sun and cloud full of gull voices, the sounds of larking geese splashing in the bogs, goose talk and the song of winds. A full harvest of goslings had been gathered and were now running on the muds, once again the geese assembled along the edge of the tide and gabbled excitedly, just as swallows talk about their coming journey as they perch along the telegraph wires. The tide of life was beginning to ebb, the tide of stillness and death to creep outwards from the Pole.

On the tenth of October all the geese left the bay and an hour after their leaving it began to blow hard from the West. The gale beat upon the flanks of the travelling skeins and turned them eastwards off their course, some tried to turn back and were driven, exhausted, into the sea. Late on the night of the eleventh the geese were hundreds of miles off their course over strange country, a country of vast pine-forests and winding rivers. Soon the fir-woods gave place to a flat land, striped by long dykes that formed a silver network in the moonlight.

Manka and Grey Mantle, together with eight other geese, came down exhausted. They were the remnants of a big skein of over three hundred strong. They alighted on the foreshore of a vast inland sea where blunt-nosed barges tossed at anchor, long-pointed flags flying from their mastheads.

It was Friesland, a land of pied cattle, farms with high-pitched red roofs, dark earth, and few trees.

The muds were thronged with waders, ruffs and reeves, mallard and teal, the latter in vast companies, thousands of them in one "spring."

And still the wind blew with fury, whirling the sails of the little windmills in the dykes and blowing straw from the neat stackyards.

The geese were content to sleep in the shelter of a timber wall; they rested until dawn.

Chapter Nine
THE GOOSE NET

Yet somewhere in this friendly well-loved land of dark earth and shining dykes his old enemy lurked. Foxy Fordham, with his ratlike-tooth and heavy tube of steel which had dealt death to many of Manka's companions.

A S soon as the light had come, the geese took stock of
their surroundings.

Behind them a wall of stout timber posts stretched as far
as eye could see. And beyond the wall was a level bank, built as
only the Dutch know how to build a bank, that kept the sea from
the flat lands behind. It was the Dutchmen who had built the
banks about the Wash, but these barriers were higher and more
massive, for they had a more responsible job to do.

The timbers were black, draped with slimy weed, from the
seaward side the land was invisible, only the tips of a windmill's
sails turned slowly against the dawn sky. Dainty pied avocets
tripped the foreshore, and a little way down the tide-line three spoon-
bills were feeding in the shallow water.

Slop! slop! the tide was washing the feet of the timber wall.
The geese rose and went over the bank, passing a narrow road, a toll
gate, and a tiny draining mill, set at the end of a long, straight dyke.
They alighted on a green meadow and began to feed.

About a hundred yards distant was a farm. Its red roof was
high, indeed it seemed all roof, with its door peeping like the en-
trance to a wren's nest from under the wide eaves. Black and white
cattle were dotted about the grassy fields and packs of reeves, like
little brown mice, moved about the ploughed lands.

In the autumn Friesland is a rather drab country of dark earth and shining dykes. In the spring the meadows are golden with dandelions and bright with bulbs, though the bulk of the bulb-growing industry is on the mainland. It is a lively, colourful country then. Redshanks trill in every dyke and many-hued ruffs posture and pose before the disinterested reeves. Manka, standing on the field, was mistaken for a spoonbill by some sabot-shod labourers going to work. They stopped, however, when they saw him grazing, and discussed him among themselves.

The geese did not tarry long in Friesland. The Wash still drew them, and after a feed and rest they continued their journey, passing over the Hook of Holland where big steamers were plying and the North Sea blazed like molten brass in the dying light of the western sky.

How pleasant it was to be back once more on the old familiar meadows! Manka knew every inch of the ground as well as he knew his native Spitzbergen. Every bank was familiar, every creek, flight-line, and tree; always with him was Grey Mantle. When Manka roosted at night on the sand-bars, she was by his side, when he stalked the furrows, plucking the tender shoots of wheat, she went with him, when he flew across the sea-bank she was close astern and sometimes ahead.

They shared their days; the grey days when the clouds hung low over the sea; the frosty days when the shadows from stack and bank remained white and crisp all day; the sunny days when the fields were open and unbound.

There were more huts on the bombing range and fewer guns along the marshes, for the restrictions had driven goose hunters elsewhere. Only on the fields inland had they need to watch for guns, and out on the sandbanks there was always a danger from the stealthy punts. Manka was wise now, he remembered the night when the sinister hull of Foxy's punt came on them through the mist, belching death among the packed grey ranks. He always slept with one eye open and one ear alert, and many times sensed approaching danger and took the skeins to safety.

There was the same routine, now dearly familiar; the morning flight out from the sand-bars when the moon was young, the wheeling, and the shouted orders as the skeins came to rest upon the feeding-grounds.

Yet somewhere in this friendly, well-loved land of dark earth and shining dykes his old enemy lurked, Foxy Fordham, with his rat-like tooth and heavy tube of steel which had dealt death to many of Manka's companions.

The day after the geese arrived from Holland, Foxy was early astir. It was a mild morning, the sharp snap had passed, the gale had gone. As he walked down the lane to the sea, starlings chattered in the tops of the ash trees bordering the road, clappering their bills and filling the air with curious rushing music. Foxy stood awhile and listened to one of them mimicking Billy's whistle, the peculiar whistle which he always used when herding his flocks. It was a perfect imitation.

Foxy did not know the geese had come in, and it was not until he was nearly at Mudhorse creek, that he heard the geese out on the sandbanks. He watched the skeins go in over the bank and it was not long before he saw the white spot, which was Manka, leading a skein of twenty pinks over the sea-wall.

The knotted hand, crooked round the stock of his gun, tightened until the knuckles showed white. Damned if it wasn't the white goose again, safe and sound as ever!

He watched them go over Mellons Platt, wheel, break, and lower, and finally vanish below the level of the sea-wall. As he went home after a fruitless "flight" he saw a vast flock of sheep "baaing" and bunching along the top of the bank, and behind them the sturdy figure of Billy.

"See the white goose agin, Foxy?"

"Ah, I did, Billy, same old white 'un and no mistake about it, maybe I'll get 'im this winter if they stay around."

Billy did not reply. His dog had wandered off on the marsh. He whistled (the peculiar whistle) and the beast came slinking back and sat down behind the men, looking up at Billy with patient eyes, full of adoration. Billy smiled.

"Yes, allus said you'd get 'im, didn't you, but 'e's a wily old beggar. Look 'ow he got away from Willow'ills; beats me 'ow 'e ever escaped."

"Simple," said Foxy, "Mr. Comfrey never pinioned 'im; I told 'im 'e'd lose 'im."

The shepherd moved off after his sheep, for they were beginning to wander along the bank. "Never mind, Foxy, you'll get 'im if you keep on a-tryin', stick to 'un, Foxy!"

For a long time Foxy leant on the wooden bridge, puffing at his pipe. Below him, on the bed of the creek, he could see a large dab, of over a pound weight, lying on the mud. Any other eye than Foxy's would have missed it, so closely did it harmonize with its surroundings. He opened his big clasp knife and sidled down the bank crab-wise. The fish was hidden for a moment in a cloud of mud, but when the obscurity billowed away he saw the big fish lying just below him. He edged within striking distance and then with a lightening thrust impaled the fish on the point of his knife and threw it kicking on to the crab grass. It was a fine catch and would make Foxy a tasty breakfast.

On the way down the lane he saw the grey blobs on the plough and a white blob sitting all by itself on a furrow ridge.

Three days later the geese moved to Willowhills.

The skein came low over Comfrey's farm, and he himself, now quite recovered from his accident, saw Manka as he led the skein down on to the big field. He had been furious when he had heard of the white goose's escape and blamed himself for not pinioning

Manka as soon as he had been caught. In his excitement he called out his wife. She was in the kitchen rolling out pastry, a buxom pink woman with arms like thighs.

"Well, what is it?"

"There's the white goose back again, the one that got away from the pen, he's down with a lot more pinks on the hundred-acre."

"You won't get him again," said Mrs. Comfrey, "once bit, twice shy!"

"We'll see about that, Clara. Tell you what, I'll net him!"

Comfrey went to the barn and looked at the net. It had been repaired and was in good working order. He'd get Foxy over at once and rig it up on the hundred-acre. He found that worthy paunching a hare behind the shed where once Manka had been a prisoner.

"Foxy, the white goose's back, went over my yard this morning. They're all feeding on the big field!"

"Ah, I seed 'im," replied Foxy without looking up. With a skilful flick he disembowelled the hare and the clucking hens rushed for the steaming spoils.

"Well, Foxy, we're going to catch him again, and this time he's not going to get away!"

They went back to the farm and scouted through the orchard.

"There you are, Foxy, behind the stack in the corner. Take the glass. It's the white goose, isn't it?"

Foxy rested the telescope on the top rail of the fence and screwed his eye. He looked a long time. Then he shifted the glass and peered with his other eye. At first he only saw the blurred outline of the stack and distant field, then a misty plover picking at the plough, almost standing on its head. One more twist and the picture became clear. It was Manka, sure enough. He was feeding away from the main gaggle with a little grey goose close behind him, the bright morning sun shining on him, throwing a shadow across the plough.

Foxy shut up the glass with a double snap.

"Ah, it's 'im, Mr. Comfrey. It's 'im, sure enough!"

They went back across the orchard, kicking the puckered rotten apples that still lay among the tangled wet grass. The geese in the pen cackled as they passed. When they got to the barn they pulled the net out into the yard and for a long while stood looking at it. If the geese continued to use Willowhills for the next day or two there was a remote chance they might catch Manka.

When the geese went back to the sea at midday the two men walked over the field and examined the ground. The geese had been feeding eighty yards out from the stack and the field was plastered with droppings. All about were little blades of wheat half pulled out, with their tops bitten off and the marks of goose paddles were everywhere on the soft, wet soil. It would be feasible to bring the trip wire across the field to the stacks, which formed an excellent hide.

That evening they lugged the net through the orchard on to the hundred-acre, not across the field, but round by the headland. Had they taken it over the wet soil it would have left marks, and Manka would have seen the tell-tale signs. It worked on the same principle as the old plover-catchers' nets. It was seventeen feet wide by eighteen long with a strong pole at either end. A steel wire, stretched over the end of the poles was the release, and the "trip" wire was taken across to the stacks and covered over with potato haulms.

It was quite dark by the time the men had finished, stars were coming out over the black roofs of the farm buildings. As they walked back to the farm, mallard passed over, quite invisible, their passage betrayed by their whistling whisper of wings. In the farmhouse kitchen Mrs. Comfrey had prepared an appetizing meal; home-cured ham, cured in the way a ham should be cured, sweet yet dry to the palate. There were two tankards of beer and a home/made loaf to which Foxy did ample justice.

On his way back to his cottage Foxy stopped on the bank and stared out towards the dark mystery of the sandbanks. No goose called, only the low throbbing of the sea came on the wind. Whether it was the strength of Comfrey's beer, or excitement as to what the morrow would bring forth, Foxy could not sleep. He listened to the wind blowing round the house, and somehow he found himself straining his ears for the sound of geese. Where had the white goose been since he last saw him topping the wire that summer night? He had never believed that Manka would come back again. Some/where, out on those sandbanks now, was Manka, an unsuspecting Manka, who knew nothing of the net waiting to catch him on Willowhills.

At six a.m. next morning Foxy hammered on the farmhouse door, bump! bump! A tornado of barks burst out, as the dog in the yard heard a stranger. Soon a yellow glow appeared on the ceiling of an upper room and Comfrey's unshaven face peered out. "Right, Foxy, I'll be down in a minute!"

After a stiff whisky and a mouthful of food the men started out for the hundred/acre. It was still pitch dark as they crossed the orchard, sticks snapped underfoot and Comfrey struck his eye against a branch. Foxy, experienced poacher and used to moving in the dark, never trod on a twig or scratched his clothes. Both men carried guns; if they failed to catch Manka they would shoot him.

Peewits called sharply as they followed the headland round to the ricks. With the aid of a flashlight they examined the net and set the spring. All was soon ready and there was nothing to do but to await the coming of the geese.

The dawn was long in greying. The two men sat down between

the stacks, covering their legs with hay, for the morning was cold, and talked to one another in quiet undertones. In the loose straw the wind rustled, overhead a duck passed out to the sea.

"Suppose 'e don't come nigh the net, Mr. Comfrey, shall I shoot 'un?"

"We'll get him alive if we can," said Comfrey, "a dead albino isn't much use to me; he's worth three times as much alive and kicking."

Foxy had waited for many a dawn but never had a vigil been so exciting. It seemed hours before the distant farm and the willow trees round the pond took shape, but at last they grew distinct. Slowly the sky grew brighter and birds began to move about. From the farm a cockerel began to crow.

"Ole cock a crowin', shan't be long now," whispered Foxy.

Distant wavering spots of light passed along the road as labourers cycled to work. More mallard passed over, "whi! whi! whi!" but they were still invisible. Soon they could discern the dim field, and, near the stacks, the length of wire half hidden in the rusty potato haulms.

Then with a rush the light came. It was a cloudy dawn.

"All the better if it ain't a bright mornin'," said Foxy. "They won't see the net so well."

More mallard passed, visible now, with outstretched necks, bottle-shaped, speeding against the dull sky in little compact bunches of five and six. There was a sense of great movement in the upper sky; for miles along the coast other ducks were likewise speeding for the sandbanks over the waking countryside.

"'Ere come the gulls!" whispered Foxy.

They came at first in twos and threes, dead over the farm, and for fully twenty minutes they passed, oaring themselves along in a sleepy manner, speaking one to another with sharp grating sounds.

All detail was clear now. The men heard the "baaing" of sheep from the sea-wall as Billy busied himself with the flocks. Then came curlew in little parties. They alighted on the big field in front and ignored the net; many settled well within the catching area. It was not until eight o'clock that the sound of the geese came to the waiting men.

At first the sound was far away and intermittent and then it grew louder. They saw two small skeins coming in over the bank and a third from Mellons Platt. They wheeled high over the stack and then with twisting, side-slipping rush they alighted on the centre of the hundred-acre, eighty yards from the catching area. More and more skeins came in, the sky was striped with them, and all came down on the big field. As yet there was no sign of Manka. Then Foxy's elbow nudged Comfrey in the ribs.

Manka was sitting among the other geese already on the field! He had come in behind them, over the stacks, and neither man had seen him arrive. Close beside him was Grey Mantle, both were within five yards of the catching area.

Down in the straw two hearts beat quickly and Foxy's hand tightened on the trip wire.

"Don't pull till he's well inside the area," whispered Comfrey, "he wants another five yards yet!"

Manka stood without moving, his back to the stacks, looking towards the farm. What was in his mind? Was he thinking of past experiences, of his days of captivity, the pacings by the wire?

Close beside him was Grey Mantle, likewise watchful. Then Manka began to feed, but alas for the men, not towards the catching area but away from it. There were fully a dozen geese within the sweep of the net and Foxy's fingers itched to pull. But there was a chance Manka would turn and feed towards them. Now and again one goose with upraised wings and extended neck would run at another. More geese passed across the fatal area, all feeding, all unsuspecting. Manka was now fifteen yards down-field and every step was taking him farther away. Foxy swore.

"Jest our luck, ain't it, the wily ——, we ain't goin' to catch 'im now."

At that moment another goose ran at Manka, who skipped to

one side, turned round, and faced the stacks. The men could almost feel those sharp little eyes scanning their hiding-places and Comfrey nudged Foxy with his elbow.

Step by step Manka came nearer, feeding cheek to cheek with Grey Mantle. Another step or two and they would be under the net. Other geese came with them. Foxy's heart was hammering so hard he felt almost faint with excitement.

"Shall I pull?" breathed Foxy.

Comfrey nodded.

Among the potato haulms the steel cable stirred like a snake, and the square of net rose and fell. It seemed to rise straight up into the air and sink again. The air was full of the thunder of rising wings and wild cacklings.

But as the men burst out from the straw Manka passed low over their heads, his little beady eye looking down at them eagerly. Foxy swore and snatched up his gun, and as it came to his shoulder Manka passed behind the stack. Only a tuft of straw flew from the top.

Out in the field there was a heaving under the net, a beating of grey wings, and wild squawks.

They ran over and pulled out three frightened geese. One had had its wing broken by the pole as it swung over, and as Comfrey ran after it Foxy secured the survivors.

The last goose he pulled from the meshes was Grey Mantle.

Chapter Ten
THE WIDOWER

Manka was now in the prime of his life. He weighed six and a half pounds and was a match for the oldest gander on the bluffs. He could take his pick from the geese on the ledges and none dare dispute his claims.

WHEN they took Grey Mantle back to the pen, Comfrey handed a knife to Foxy and nodded towards her wing. The latter pinioned her by cutting the wing-joint, rather a painful process for poor Grey Mantle, but Comfrey was taking no chances.

"*She* won't get over no wire," said Foxy, standing up and shutting the clasp knife with a snick. "Pity we hadn't done the same to the white goose. I reckon, e'd 'a been 'ere now."

Next morning they took Grey Mantle to the hundred-acre, and tying a leather strap around her leg, pegged her out on the field. Once more they hid in the stacks and watched the dawn come over the sea.

As Comfrey well knew, it would be the merest chance if Manka returned to the field where he had been so badly scared; however, it was worth the trial. Soon after daybreak the men heard the geese coming in, but none descended on the hundred-acre field. Once geese have been scared off a feeding-ground they will not return for weeks.

When Manka had gone back to the sea on the previous morning, he had searched miserably for Grey Mantle all down the coast. He flew over to Frieston and all round the margin of the Wash. That night he left the skeins and roosted by himself far out on the sands with only wigeon for company. As soon as it was light he searched the marshes by Mudhorse creek, and having no answer to his calls came back to Willowhills. His sharp eyes soon picked out the half-concealed wire leading to the net, he also saw suspicious movements between the stacks.

Yet the ties between Grey Mantle and Manka were so strong that they overcame distrust and fear. The watching men saw him circling the field, calling to his goose on the ground. But he would not come near the net or the stacks. He pitched a long way out in the centre of the field, and was puzzled when she would not join him.

After a while he rose and flew away over the orchard and the men picked up the exhausted Grey Mantle and carried her back to the pen. She had struggled so violently on the ground that she had strained the tendon in her leg. They put her down and she hobbled away to one corner of the pen.

In the days that followed, Comfrey saw Manka about Willowhills nearly every day. Frequently the gander circled the farm, calling, and Grey Mantle replied. The other geese in the pen worked themselves into a great state of excitement when they saw Manka flying overhead, but he kept well away and out of range. It seemed useless to try and net the white gander again, for he had been badly scared. It was only Grey Mantle that held him to the marshes about the Wash; the rest of the geese had gone to the Essex marshes for a change of air, and he should have been with them. No longer did he join the skeins, he was a bachelor again, as he was in the days when he haunted Starvation Point.

That season had been mild up to late November. Then Comfrey awoke one morning to find the world white, and long icicles hanging from the gutters of the big barn. Puffed-out blackbirds and thrushes crawled about like autumn flies, and sat about the yard begging for crumbs. The grey wood-pigeons, unable to get at the young wheat, raided Comfrey's winter greens.

The geese went away, only Manka stayed, a white bird in a white land. Foxy often saw him flying in from the sea; but Manka never used the same flight-line twice in succession, and never the same feeding-ground.

One morning, two days after the full of the moon, Comfrey went out as usual to feed the geese. Grey Mantle had settled down well in her captivity, and came with the other geese when he rattled the galvanized iron bucket. Wild geese are usually adaptable birds, and Grey Mantle was no exception. When Comfrey came up to the pen he nearly dropped the bucket. Manka was standing at the far end with Grey Mantle by his side. And stranger still, when he saw Comfrey, he did not fly, but walked slowly away with erect neck to the hump of trodden mud above the pond.

Comfrey was so nonplussed he did not know what to do. He could have shot Manka with ease, but he wanted him alive. It seemed so absurd that Manka, though in the pen, was still free. Comfrey did the wisest thing. He did not disturb Manka but went back to the farm and told his wife. From an upper window they could see the goose-pen and for a long time they watched Manka standing above the pond. He never moved, but remained watchful, with erect head.

After a while Comfrey decided he would throw some grain into the pen. He quietly opened the gate and put the bucket down. When the geese saw him coming they came running towards him. Manka sprang into the air and flew away towards the marshes.

Comfrey was now quite certain Manka would come back and he racked his brains for some method of catching him.

It may seem strange to those unversed in the ways of wild geese to understand why a wary bird like Manka should have returned to the farm where he had spent months of captivity. But for a long time he had been familiar with the pen and its surroundings. Even the appearance of Comfrey did not unduly alarm him, for he had seen him so many times before coming along the same path at the same time. And his love for Grey Mantle was strong.

If Comfrey could once have got Manka to feed, he might easily have trapped him. Doped corn seemed the easiest solution, a method suggested by Foxy, who had caught many a pheasant by grain soaked in whisky.

But when Comfrey went out next morning there was no Manka in the pen, and he almost wished he had shot him.

"Keep feedin' 'em," said Foxy, "'e'll come back." They tried it. They even scattered feed liberally about the wire, but Manka did not come again. The white goose had not left the district; every day Foxy saw him either down on the tide-line, or feeding on the fields about Mellons Platt. The snow still lay on the ground and Manka must have had a hard job to find pickings, yet he remained.

The moon cast patterns of shadow from the apple trees in the orchard. Behind each rick was a pool of dark shade in which the rats ran. Tucked up in the straw, snug as dormice, were sparrows and finches. There is nothing like hay for warmth, and the little birds knew this from experience.

In the early hours, Grey Mantle stood by the wire looking towards the sea. On moonlight nights the geese were always restless, even those pinioned geese in the pen. They chattered and called to the passing skeins, for they longed to join them, up there among the cold stars.

Grey Mantle paced the same beat that Manka had once paced, up and down, up and down, along the walls of wire. Liberty for Grey Mantle had gone for ever, she could never fly again.

When the shadow of the farm wheeled so that it lay across the midden in the yard Grey Mantle heard a well-loved "Ank! ank!" from far beyond the sea-wall. She answered, and soon afterwards a white shadow, like a great owl, dropped over the apple trees and landed in the pen. For five nights Manka came in this way whilst man, the enemy, slept. Within the pen all was indistinct in the moonlight. Down by the pond the barnacle geese showed up vividly, and there were black shadows thrown from the big greylag geese as they walked about under the trees.

Manka wondered why Grey Mantle would not follow him when he left the pen. Several times he hopped over the wire and stood on the field where the old leaves of autumn lay in drifts down each furrow. But she would not come—she would not come.

The next day, Comfrey found a white feather in the pen, it might have been from any of the geese, but it gave him an idea. Perhaps Manka was coming at night under the moon. It might be worth waiting up to see.

So that night, he watched from the upper window. Though the moon was late in rising and gave but feeble light, he could see the pen and the geese quite plainly. Soon after midnight Comfrey saw something white slip over the roof of the barn and land among the other geese in the pen. It was Manka, without a doubt.

Comfrey then made up his mind. All efforts to trap Manka had been useless, he would shoot him. He went downstairs and got his gun, for the pen was in range of the window.

When he got back to the upper room Manka was still there, close to the edge of the little pond at the far end of the pen. Unfortunately there were a lot of other geese with him and Comfrey valued his birds too much to sacrifice any of them needlessly. So he quietly pushed up the window and waited until Manka should walk away from the others.

It was a long time before he did so. At length Comfrey saw him climb the bank above the water, and stand looking towards the farm.

Slowly he pushed the barrel out of the window and edged the butt of the gun up to his shoulder. The moonlight caught the barrel. Manka instantly saw the gleam. He sprang upwards and was lost against the blue-green sky. Comfrey held his fire. He would wait for another chance.

But Manka never came back to Willowhills. Even his love for Grey Mantle could not draw him, and Comfrey spent several fruit-less nights waiting with his gun under the apple trees.

During the new year many geese came in to the marshes or the fields but the white goose was not among the skeins. The long winter dragged on to spring, to the time when the golden crocus buds (last year's sunlight re-born) pierced the dark earth on the borders of Mellons Platt.

Once again the rooks got busy over the last year's nests, and in the new reed-jungles, down the dykes, mallard swam with their broods. The little striped balls of fluff shot about like water beetles in the wake of their mother as she threaded her way among the tangled herbage. There was a new smell in the air, especially in the early morning and early evenings, a scent of growing things pushing through the soil, of fresh grass trampled by sheep. On a farm the evidence of spring is more insistent than elsewhere. The first swallows hawk about the outbuildings, the bleat of lambs sounds all day.

Again came the long twilights, when the day lingers in the sky long after sundown, and there is a call of the open road, magnetic as the romance of autumn.

No longer did puddles shine down the coast drove, the March winds had sucked them dry; the increasing warmth of the sun quickly absorbed the moisture that all winter long had soaked the fields and hedges. When the plough turned at the end of the furrow a cloud of dried dust drifted, the blackthorn was white again. Billy was up with the lark. There were many larks about those flat lands. They climbed into the March skies with little flips that bore them upwards until the whole area about the Wash was spread like a map below them and Billy's sheep showed no bigger than wasp grubs.

It is no use pretending that Grey Mantle mourned for Manka, for this is not a story of human beings. She had forgotten him long ago. In the pen there was abundance of food and plenty of company, but she yearned for freedom and the high skyroads that led across the sea. With the rising of the sap of Life she had mated with one of the other pinioned pinks in the pen, and Comfrey even dared to hope the impossible might happen, and that they might breed.

During the middle of March, skeins of geese passed high over Willowhills, some so high that they were scarcely visible. Even the singing larks were below them and the ground was veiled from them by misty vapours. Yet the pinioned birds in the pen knew of their passing and ran up and down by the wire walls.

You can sail all the way from Northampton to the sea, now they have widened the Nene. The river flows through broad water-meadows, black poplars dot the valley floor, and picturesque stone villages, with broach-spired churches, cluster the low, swelling hills on either side. Fishing matches are held there on Sunday afternoons and rows of patient figures, glued to camp-stools, huddle along the banks watching with pathetic intensity the slender white quills swaying in the current. The fishermen are as serious as little boys fishing for tiddlers in a mill brook. Their womenfolk sometimes bring them tea in thermos flasks, inwardly smiling at the male who never really grows up. At Wisbech the river begins to feel the sea, and the banks are scoured by the arm of the tide, redshanks and gulls haunt the fields on either side. There the country is as flat as Holland, there are few trees and no picturesque villages snuggle among wooded hill-sides. An ancient land of abbeys and fine churches, where herons flap lazily across wide skies.

Some few miles outside Northampton, beyond the range of the raw pink bungalows, the water-meadows are remote. In winter they flood, till in a wet season the water lies like a succession of shining lakes for miles, so that the valley is one vast broad.

To these flooded lands the wigeon come in thousands from the East Coast and under the moon the "weeho, weeho" of the drakes echoes all night through. Three half-tame swans had used this flooded valley since mid-February. They had come from an ornamental water at Tring. The rich feed in the flooded meadows was better than bread crusts. Another bird was with them, as white as they, half the size of the swans and with a short, thick neck. It was Manka. Why or how he had chosen these swans for his companions I cannot say. Since he had lost Grey Mantle he had shunned the skeins on the coast. Maybe he had first come across the swans in the river above Wisbech and when they moved higher up the river he went with them.

All March he kept them company, feeding among the big kingcup blobs on the water-meadows and resting at night on the flood water. Many people saw Manka and thought he was a cygnet, so ignorant are the bulk of people in identifying birds. So nobody desired to kill him, and he found a peace that he had not known for months. No longer was he troubled by the roll of gun-fire at twilight, only an occasional rabbit-potter gave him cause for alarm.

It was a sunny March, with little rain and much calm weather. In the long twilights the rooks flew cawing in long lines over the quiet water-meadows, thrushes sang among the sprays of black-thorn to the accompaniment of bleating lambs.

The sound of children at play in the distant villages came across the green valley. Sometimes a herdsman passing along by the river disturbed Manka, who saw the red-brown cattle plodding towards the farms at milking-time. There were more plovers on these water-meadows than on the coast, their numbers must have run into thousands, each twilight was full of their thin crying. Manka and the swans took flights up the river, but they always pitched again within a mile or two.

On the last day of March, Manka, refreshed after this period of rest, said good-bye to his big companions and flew North. The

"Thrushes singing in the twilight"

last he saw of them was of three white spots, sitting on the flood water stained by a saffron sky. That quiet midland countryside, with its sense of coming spring and poplar-studded water-meadows, dropped astern, muffled in the dusk of coming night.

It was good-bye to England for Manka, he followed in the van of the migrating skeins, a lone white wanderer who steered unerring course for Sassen Bay.

Manka found solid ice in the bay, for it was yet early and winter still lingered. The returning sun had begun his task of unbinding the rivers and melting the snowfields, every day there were signs of the battle being won. Manka flew straight to Starvation Point. There was no dark moss as yet, all was wrapt in a bank of snow. On the point, ice-blocks were piled high in a jagged wall, full of green caverns and icicle teeth.

A bear was swimming with her cub among the floes at the mouth of the Sassendal. The cub scrambled on to an ice-floe and promptly slipped back into the water, but the mother reached down a strong, furry arm and yanked it up again by the scruff of the neck, and together they ambled away past the ruined hut, mobbed by screaming gulls.

A tired Manka pitched among the ice-blocks and folded aching wings. There was no Grey Mantle awaiting him as he had expected, but he was so weary he went to sleep, and mercifully no fox came slinking down the rocks. When he awoke he flew over to the bluffs and found geese already there, many of his old companions whom he had not seen since the early winter on the Wash.

It was a full three weeks before all the geese were back in Sassen Bay, meanwhile Manka had found another mate and had staked out his claim to a ledge on the bluffs, close to his birthplace. Both Manka's parents failed to return, some dark tragedy had overtaken them across the sea. Maybe a punt stealing up a creek had put an end to the story of their lives or they had met their death in the paling dawn, far away on some Scottish firth.

Manka was now in the prime of his life. He weighed six and a half pounds and was a match for the oldest gander on the bluffs. He could take his pick from the geese on the ledges, for none dare dispute his claims. Manka's new mate was a five-year-old, hatched on the other side of the island.

They reared a family without incident and at the end of July moulted out their flights, and for a while Manka had to run and creep again, as he did in those perilous days on the Wash. They joined the other flightless geese on the marshes by the Sassendal and waited patiently there for their new feathers to grow again.

Chapter Eleven
THE COMING OF THE SIRIUS

Among the mosses on Starvation Point were the blackened trunks of trees. They had come all the way from America on the Gulf Stream. High tides had thrown them up on the shore and so they had lain for years. So it seemed that some trees, like men, were travellers, whilst others stayed at home, rooted to the same spot all their days.

THE *Sirius* came grunting up the coast, sending a furl of water that talked among the ice-caverns at the glacier foot and set the seals a-bob like little old men. Against the background of white snowfield and floes the ship looked very black and toy-like, the smudge from her funnel drifting out across the calm sea. Gulls were weaving about her stern, some sitting on the rocking wake. One big fellow was perched right on top of the forward mast, keeping a strict watch on the galley door.

As she came abreast of Sassen Bay the beat of her engines slowed and ceased, small ice-floes scraped and tinkled down her rusty sides and the dead smooth water in her wake was spotted with iridescent oil bubbles.

Her captain was a tough old Dane with a fierce beard and bristling moustache. Through a pair of binoculars he was scanning the desolate opening of the bay, his bushy brows pushed over the rims of the eye-pieces.

The rumble of the anchor came echoing back from the mountains in muffled roarings that set all the loomeries white with screaming fowl.

Three Englishmen stood on the bridge by the Captain's side. Wilbur, slight and fair-haired, Sutherland, a tall, loose-limbed Angus man, and Bobby Mellon, M.B.O.U., who had more money than his many friends knew what to do with. He it was who had chartered the ship on this voyage of scientific exploration.

"We'll stay here, Captain, for a couple of days and have a look round, what do you say?"

"Goot, Mr. Mellon, but the ice, we watch heem, ice no good. One night he come, wake up next day, *Sirius* fast. We stay here till spring. Wind in bad quarter just now."

"Well, we'll chance it, Captain, I must go up that valley. What's that on the point there?"

"Ah—he, hut, built years ago, many years, the Dutchmen build it. They hunt whales here, they die there on the point. Bad place, Mister Mellon. You see skeletons there, poor Dutchmen; they lie there, starve to death, bears play with them now. Bears play with us if ice come."

"Good," said Mellon briskly, "that settles it; we'll camp up the valley." "Damned if I want any bears playing bowls with my skull," said Wilbur, "Holfessen's always so damned pessimistic."

Mellon, his glasses glued to his eyes, saw three birds flying over the mosses.

"Geese over there," he said, "maybe we shall see what they are if we explore the valley."

An hour later a boat put off from the *Sirius*. It appeared no bigger than a seal as it passed among the ice-blocks. Inquisitive gulls and kittiwakes followed in a cloud; it was long since a boat had come to Sassen Bay. Guillemots rode the waves like little pied boats and goggling seals rolled off the floes and bobbed up yards away, seeming to be sitting on arm-chairs under the water, or like old gentlemen in Turkish baths. One of the sailors jumped out as the boat grounded among the rocks and threw an anchor down into the black moss, the men stepped out.

"God! What a country!" Mellon stood gazing in awe towards the high rampart of the Colorado range, hard white against the grey sky. Over the marshes lay a mist that hid the upper neck of the valley in a mysterious veil. The men picked their way across the moss to the hut, their rubber boots squelching in the spongy ground. Wilbur, a little way past the hut, was shouting and waving his arm.

"Wilbur must have found the Dutchmen," said Mellon. "Let's go and see."

"Just look at this." Wilbur was balancing a femur in his hand. "Ground must have been too hard to bury him, I suppose."

There were other oddments among the stones, coins and an old rusty gun. Wilbur picked up a coin. It was worn smooth, but part of the date was visible, 17—, the rest was obliterated. He slipped it into his pocket and turned to look towards the valley. A dark storm-cloud was sweeping down across a snowfield and fitful darts of rain stung the faces of the men, like pricking needles. Northwards there was a jangle and growl of ice and the sea was a lead colour, oily, and rocking slightly.

"Ugh!" grunted Wilbur, "shouldn't like to have to spend a winter here with the Dutchmen; might be a bit lonely!"

"And a bit chilly," added the Scotchman. "Where are we going to camp, Bobby?"

"Oh! up the valley somewhere, let's get going; tell Hans."

"Suppose that means we've got to get our gear over the marshes; they look pretty good from here," said Sutherland.

"They are," answered Mellon, going over the ground with his glasses. "And what's more, Sandy, my boy, they're simply lousy with geese! Just take a look through these glasses."

Sutherland stood a long time watching the geese. In the silence came the far cry of gulls and faint banging of ice.

"You're right, Bobby, they're geese all right, but I can't just see what they are, maybe whitefronts."

They set off across the rocks towards the marshes, and as they went, Wilbur slipped two cartridges into the breech of his shot-gun. "Goose for supper, boys," said Mellon from the rear.

"Won't get near 'em," said Wilbur, his eyes on the distant

blobs that were scattered over the marsh, "not if I know wild geese; we'll have to bellycrawl to 'em, I expect."

"Look!" exclaimed Mellon in an excited voice, touching Wilbur on the arm, "what's that running among the rocks?"

Wilbur turned about and the gun came to his shoulder. The two men held their breath while the gun swung and then a drill of blue smoke jetted from the muzzle and the echoes went clamouring up the valley, setting every gull on the wing for miles. The ledges of the cliffs spouted birds and the air was full of plaintive keenings.

When the men walked across they saw a leg sticking out from behind a boulder, Wilbur bent down and lifted a fox by the brush.

"Phew! what a beauty," exclaimed Mellon, "I'll skin him when we get to camp."

"The geese aren't up," said Wilbur, flicking the smoking case on the black moss, "that's funny. They've probably never heard a gun before, here."

They left the body of the fox on top of a flat rock to be collected by the sailor following behind with the tent and gear. After a few steps Wilbur turned his head and saw two big gulls had alighted by the fox's body and were regarding it with greedy eyes.

He rammed another cartridge into the breech and fired two shots. One gull fell down the side of the rock, the other flew raggedly over the marsh to twirl and fall dead on to a snow-patch. "That skin won't be worth sixpence if you leave it there, Wilbur," said Mellon.

"No. Suppose you're right. Better tell Hans to dump the stuff here and we'll come back for it. We can hide the skin under the rock."

When the sailor came up with them, carrying the tent on his back, they told him to return to the ship.

"Watch the ice, Hans," said Mellon, lighting a cigarette, "and if things look sticky, sound the siren and have a boat ready on the shore."

"So, yes, I understand, sir, we will watch."

The three young men continued their way along the foot of the slope. It was rough going among the jumbled rocks and in the snow-bogs they sank up to the knee. Wilbur turned for the higher ground and found the going better, though at times he had to make wide detours to avoid massive blocks of fallen ice.

All this time the geese on the marsh had been walking away towards the Sassendal, like a flock of domestic geese being driven to a fair. Now and again a goose would jump into the air as if endeavouring to fly.

"They're not whitefronts," muttered Wilbur, taking another look through the glasses, "they're pinks, the whole lot of them. Good many goslings with them too, some not out of down. Let's pitch the tent and go after them later."

"Good idea," said Sutherland.

Some hours later they had pitched the tent close to the bluffs within earshot of the waterfall. From the tent door they looked out over the marshes to the river where the shining network of the gutters showed in all directions against the dark tones of the moss. Dark clouds hid the Colorado range and the bay was wrapt in fog.

Mellon, gun across shoulder, climbed above the camp to scan the bay. There was no sign of the ship, for the fog was thickening. Away from his companions he had a sudden sense of the terrifying loneliness that lay upon this land, an elemental feeling hard to define, the threat of a wilderness antagonistic to life.

Dimly he realized the awful Arctic winter, when the very rocks complained under the grip of the frost, when the skin of the earth shrivelled as if touched with fire, banging like cannon. He saw the beginning of things before life came to the seas and the land, the ghastly sense of tons of inert and blind matter, devoid of all warmth and life, appalling as outer space.

That July evening the country seemed especially forbidding. Cautiously he crossed a glacier, once slipping waist-deep in a miniature crevasse.

Below him was an arm of the sea, full of ice-floes. Parties of long-tailed duck were bobbing and larking in a pool close inshore. As he watched they all rose as though something had scared them. They flew across the ice and settled in another open pool on the far side of a floe. Mellon, watching through his glasses, saw a round, shiny knob emerge where the ducks had been. As he watched, it vanished. Beyond the floe the ducks began to swim about once more, rolling on their sides and splashing the water. Again there was a sudden commotion, and this time all flew away, save one which flapped desperately for a minute and then was drawn under. A few minutes later he saw a seal climb out on an ice-floe and begin eating something. It was the body of a duck.

There was a good smell of cooking in the air when Mellon returned to camp and he found Sutherland plucking a goose. It was a young bird with undeveloped wings, Sutherland had caught it below the bluffs.

When they turned in, after a yarn and smoke round the camp-fire, they heard the murmur of the waterfall, which lulled them to drowsy contentment. Wilbur lay awake thinking of many things. The homely sound of the fall recalled sleepy summer afternoons on the "Backs," redolent with lime trees, and the "unforgettable, unforgotten" smell of the river. That world seemed a long way away.

The continuous sound of the water reminded him that all streams, however small, find their ultimate endings in the sea, even the little brooklets of mid-England, that wound through primrose-studded banks and green spinneys.

Next morning Wilbur and Mellon set off to explore the marshes

towards the north, leaving Sutherland to flay the fox, with seven
attendant glaucous gulls standing like vultures on the near-by rocks.

"There's a white bird over there," said Wilbur, as the two men
examined the marshes through their glasses. "It isn't a gull, for
it's too big; what the devil is it?"

"Looks like a snow goose."

"Rot!"

"Well, look at him."

"By Jove! you're right," exclaimed Wilbur, "let's try a stalk."

They set off across the marsh, sinking above their ankles in the
spongy moss.

The geese saw the men coming a long way off and began to
walk away in a herd. Manka was in the middle of a gaggle of
about twenty birds, and it was hard to get a clear view of him.
After a while the men gained on the geese. They expected any
moment that all the birds would fly, but still the geese walked away
before them, their necks clustered in a grove.

As the men drew nearer, all the geese began to run. Mellon,
singling out the white goose, managed to separate him from the
rest of the gaggle. Manka went doubling away between the big
hummocks and disappeared behind a snow-cornice.

When Mellon gained the spot Manka was nowhere to be seen.
Directly in front was a small glacier. A stream flowing across it
had cut a deep channel in the ice. All about were tumbled rocks
and ice-blocks and large areas of rotten snow. For some time
Mellon searched the rocks, his gun at the ready. It seemed incredible that the goose should vanish in this way and he almost
began to think that Manka could fly after all. Perhaps he had
crossed the stream and was hiding in the scattered rocks beyond.

Mellon worked slowly up the bank of the stream, looking for
a place to cross. As he got higher up the slope he passed under
hanging masses of ice, some with jagged teeth poised to strike. At

last the stream narrowed, pent up between icy walls and flowing smoothly, crystal clear. It appeared only a few feet deep and easily wadable. Mellon let himself down gingerly into the current, his elbows on the ice-ledge. Without warning the ice suddenly gave way with a soft scrunch, his gun slipped out of his hand, and a second later the swift current had plucked him from the side and he was rolling and spluttering down the bed of the stream.

It was with difficulty he managed to pull himself out, and as he caught hold of an overhanging rock Manka jumped from under a ledge, almost between his legs. He saw the white goose running swiftly as a stag towards the river, but he was too exhausted to follow. Already his clothes were freezing on him and were as hard as boards. His precious Purdey, that had cost him over a hundred guineas, was gone, and though he retraced his steps up the bank of the stream there was no sign of it. The gun must have been swept down with the current to the deeper water beyond the glacier foot. Mellon gave up the hunt and started to walk back over the rim of the hill not in the happiest frame of mind. A wind had arisen. It began to blow hard from the north, fluttering the dead poppy-heads on the mosses, tossing the snow buntings about like scraps of paper, and piping among the cornices with a mournful dirge. Suddenly, from the bay came the wail of the *Sirius'* siren, "Mooomp! Mooooomp!" The wind caught the sound and whistled it away, and Mellon, shivering and exhausted, again felt the antagonism of this desolate island. He would be glad when they had left.

It was a relief when Wilbur's head bobbed over the sky-line. He was waving his gun and carrying two dead geese by the paddles. "Mellon! Mellon! We've got to strike camp; the ice is coming into the bay!"

Manka, sitting among the black mosses by the river, raised his long neck and watched the two pygmy figures toiling over the ridge above him. They moved as slowly as beetles and their heads bobbed a moment on the sky-line then sank from sight. He shook his feathers and began to feel among his quills where new flights were beginning to grow.

Wedged across the walls of ice in the torrent was Mellon's gun, six feet under in the gin-clear water. It lies there still.

The wind that had nearly trapped the *Sirius* increased to a gale during the next few hours. The ship had just managed to slip through to open water, with an hour to spare, and the smudge from her funnel sank over the rim of the white horizon. So much ice and severe weather was unusual at that time of year, but the Arctic plays queer tricks on unwary mariners.

Every evening now, the bay froze over with an elastic skin of ice. Under this skin the sea heaved, but the ice-film did not break, and even when the sun shone at midday the film remained.

One darkening evening towards the end of August a half-submerged object came bumping on the rocks by Starvation Point. It was a capsized boat. "Scrunch, scrunch," it rubbed against the smooth rocks and then the tide swung it free and it drifted out again into the sunset, breaking the skin of ice into wafers.

Among the mosses on Starvation Point were the blackened trunks of trees. They had come all the way from America on the Gulf Stream. High tides had thrown them up the shore and so they had lain for years. So it seemed that some trees, like men, were travellers, while others stayed at home, rooted in the same place.

Now, in the first week in September, Manka was fit and well. His flights had grown again, his life depended on those strong notched vanes at the tips of his wings.

A maimed wing in Spitzbergen meant certain death in the

great cold. Every day now this cold was stalking ever nearer. It only needed a stooping falcon or the snap of a fox's jaws to bring disaster.

Once again the ice-blink shivered over North East Land and the geese made ready to be gone. And on the twentieth of September they left Spitzbergen and headed once more along the old highway.

Chapter Twelve
THE WANDERING LIFE

Four successive springs whitened the blossom of the apple-trees at Willow-hills, and later, red-cheeked apples dropped to the grass in the waspy days of August, for the farm remained without a tenant. The farm buildings were silent, save for the chirp of sparrows and whistle of starlings; the pen where Manka had once been held a prisoner rotted away, only a few upright posts remained and a strand or two of rusty wire.

FROM cliff and marsh the birds had flown, another summer sun had put in his sickle and reaped a bountiful harvest of life; the fruits of five months courtship, nest build, ings, and incubation, were safely away on countless wings.

Such a short while ago the ledges of the loomeries on the cliffs had been teeming with thousands of birds, both old and young. Now little remained but the splashes of lime on the rocks and an occasional bird, a gull or a skua, perched on some whitened pinnacle that overlooked the ice-strewn sea.

From among the boulders upon many a high slope, snow bunting fledglings had flown, the empty, fouled nests lined with feathers were the only signs remaining. From the mosses, redpolls, phalaropes, and purple sandpipers had hatched and gone away. All had departed, following the sun.

Manka and his companions did not fly direct to the Wash. During the latter half of their journey they met adverse winds which blew them to the eastwards.

Manka therefore shaped a course for Scotland and twenty-nine hours after they left Sassendal they sighted the bright scattered jewels of Perth and Dundee and smelt the homely heathery hills once again.

They found a great company on the sandbanks of the Tay; more than two thousand geese were assembled there. Such a number may seem unbelievable to those who do not live in districts where wild geese congregate, but far greater numbers are sometimes seen in the autumn, at their appointed stations.

There were geese from Iceland and Greenland, as well as from Spitzbergen, and mingled with them were greylags, some, British birds, hatched in the wilder parts of Sutherland and the Summer Isles. For the next few weeks they fed in company with hundreds of others on the farms about the foothills and the Carse.

Once again Manka heard the murmur of the Inchgarvie burn, a sound that must have reminded him of his native land.

Rob soon noted Manka flighting out in the mornings from Curlew Bay. Though he ambushed on the long breakwater, he never had the chance of a shot. And when Manka crossed the mountains Rob chased him there, his motor-cycle making heavy weather of the snow on the pass. His friend the grieve, who owned the farm on which the geese fed, was a distant relation.

Many vigils did Rob spend on the snow-covered field by the flood flash, lying out on the white, hard surface with a dust sheet over him. And though he shot several "pinks," Manka was not among them. After a while all the geese came back to the Carse and used the river. Rob prayed for wind. At last it came, a full gale from the West, and the reed-beds that a day before were empty of duck, were alive with fowl of all kinds. The reason was that the sea was so rough they could not sleep on the waves and the wild weather drove them to the shelter of the river.

At dawn, under a half-moon, Rob stalked the reedbeds by Curlew Bay. The strong wind beat the reeds until their dead plumed heads bowed almost to the ground and the continuous rustling drowned the sound of Rob's stealthy footsteps through the bog. It was pitch dark, so dark that Rob's gun-barrels were invisible, but he knew these reed-beds like a book, he also knew where he would be likely to find the geese.

The great birds were right among the short reed stubbles, pulling them up by the roots to get at the hard, round bulbs of which they were so fond. He could hear them as he crawled closer, gobbling and sloshing about in the shallow water.

It was no pleasant business crawling through these reed-beds, for as he had to go on all fours he sank into the wet mud until it came well above the wrists. Rob crawled right in amongst the feeding geese, it was a thrilling experience to be so close to such wily birds. Some were within a yard or two of him, he could hear them walking about, and the sucking sound of their paddles in the mire. If he had stretched out his gun he could have touched the nearest bird. He had once grabbed a goose by the legs on such a morning as this. Apparently geese cannot see in the dark any more than human beings.

Rob lay down and waited for it to get light. Before day had fully come the geese would begin to go out to the river. But there would be a time, in the half-light of dawn, when he could see to shoot.

Slowly the forms of the hills grew distinct across the river, and he could see below him the dark bar of the stone breakwater against the paling river.

It seemed as if, with the coming of the light, the geese knew they must hurry up and finish their meal. The gabbling and splashings were redoubled. A foot away two geese were fighting, he could hear angry squawks and the beating of wings. Yet the geese were still invisible, they seemed to blend in an amazing way with their surroundings. Rob was by now wet to the skin and shivering with cold, he could feel his dog pressed against his side, shuddering violently, though this was partly excitement.

At last he could make out dim forms moving about ahead of

him, on all sides, and he edged the gun up in readiness to fire. Then, directly ahead, he saw a dim white shape. It appeared to be moving, yet Rob could not be quite sure. The light was exasperating, it was that light that gives to inanimate things, when regarded steadily, the appearance of movement. The more he looked the more certain he became that it was indeed a goose, *and* the white goose.

It was worth the risk, he would fire. He took careful aim and the finger tightened on the trigger. Bang! bang! the double shots broke through the cackling and the splashing of the geese. In an instant every bird was up, baying like a pack of savage hounds. But the white object did not rise. Rob walked over and found, not Manka, but an empty wooden box, bleached white by long immersion in the sea!

However, there was one goose down in the short reeds beyond, indeed it was strange that he had not killed half a dozen, for his shots had appeared to go right into the thick of the geese. Rob's number five shot had played like a hose on the box, the side was peppered with little round holes.

As for Manka, he had been far away, half a mile down the reeds, and was now heading with the rest of the skeins out towards the river. Rob stood and watched them go clamouring over the river until he lost them against the dark blue hills on the other side.

Other skeins were rising from the banks, no doubt disturbed by his shots, and were heading out to land, black lines of blobs against a sky of palest primrose.

During the next week Manka went over to Montrose, resting in the basin at night and feeding on the upland farms about Duns Dish, a circular lake high up in the hills. They frequently used this water for bathing and midday siestas, but it was more dangerous than Montrose Basin and they preferred the latter place.

Little Loch Niver

A salmon river ran into the basin at its westerly end and the waters at the mouth were alive with jumping sea trout.

All that beautiful country, from Montrose to Perth, Manka came to know as well as he knew the Wash. When the moon came to the full there was the old familiar tang in the air, the marsh froze, and the snipe in Curlew Bay were driven to the hill bogs. A great country, beloved of geese, with an ancient dignity all its own.

Winter lay like a sparkling mantle on the fir-clad hills, Spitzbergen must have seemed like a darkened room compared to this world of clean, sweet airs, full of frosty sunshine, with the Tay shining between its green valleys. The geese spent the whole of December on the river and with the new year the frost became more intense.

Hogmanay passed. Manka, feeding on Inchgarvie under the moon, heard the drink-fuddled rustics singing their way along the high road as they "first-footed" their neighbours.

There were happy journeyings to and from the river and visits to lonely lochs in the hills. One such loch was a favourite with the geese. It was remote, not even a track led thither, there were no farms within ten miles or so and only in the shooting season did figures appear on the heathery sky-line above the loch. Little Loch Niver is a blue jewel in summer, a window to the sky, the stags roar about it in the October dusk, the lordly eagle sails over. There was an island in the middle of the loch, a green place with trees and thick bushes and the ruins of a chapel.

Many days Manka and his mate went there, and after washing in the shallows by the island would wade ashore and rest awhile in the sun among the stones, lulled by the lapping of the riplets.

It was a sheltered loch. Northwards towered a high mountain, scarred deeply by centuries of sun and wind. After heavy snow, or in spring, its gutters grew thunderous and white, in the quiet nights their faint murmur echoed across the still waters.

Sometimes Manka stalked close to the ruined chapel, plucking the fine, rabbit-nibbled grass, even as other geese had stalked, six centuries before. Inside the four crumbling walls there was a tangle of bramble and blackthorn bushes that in spring topped the moss-grown walls with sprays of white blossom.

The rabbits were everywhere, they had burrows in every part of the island. How they came there in the first place was a mystery, for it seems doubtful if they could have swum across nearly half a mile of water. Close by the ruin were the remains of a cell. Its holy tenant had long since fallen asleep and lay under the altar of the chapel. In midsummer, high stinging nettles covered the floor. The old hermit had gone, but the rabbits were still there, descendants of the same rabbits that had fed on the sweet green grass in the hermit's time.

At one end of the island were seven Scotch firs, and in the tallest was a massive bundle of sticks. Years ago, ospreys built in the tree, and the proud plumed fishermen had caught the spotted trout under the very walls of the chapel. It was now many years since an osprey had perched on the dead fir bough near the nest, yet the nest remained, a perpetual monument to the skill of the architects.

Where a little burn ran in, at the shallow end of the loch, stood grey herons fishing for eels or small troutlings, and many times Manka saw them wobbling their long necks as the eels endeavoured to climb up the way they had come down.

Plenty of duck haunted the loch, and at night they flighted out over the mountain for the distant Tay. Manka, stalking by the burn, would often hear them quacking in the shallows. Lordly stags came down to the loch to drink; and sometimes they fought, tearing up the soft mosses by the water's edge.

In the quiet evenings Manka came back to this loch and found peace there. In the still mirror the reflections of the surrounding mountains were faithfully reflected and from the far end of the loch came the talk of the Boikin burn running under the arching alders. Higher up the glen it wound among tumbled rocks and entered a dark valley, a sinister place roofed over by dense trees. The echo of the water from the rocks on either side of the glen was eerie.

Occasionally a roe-deer came to drink, threading its way through the close-crowding alders.

Few birds haunted the glen, only the white-waistcoated dipper seemed unaffected by the sinister feeling of the place. Sometimes at nights the geese would be startled to full wakefulness by the unearthly cries of the Northern Divers. There were several pairs on Little Loch Niver, for they bred among the heather at one end of the island.

When the weather was hard, wild swans came over the mountains and stayed on the loch for as long as the frost lasted, "upending" in the shallow water and curving their long necks.

Wild geese sometimes choose strange feeding-ground. When the January moon came to the full, Manka and seven companions used to flight out from Little Loch Niver to an aerodrome in Angus. This aerodrome was alive with wildfowl at night, for some reason they liked the grass. Where the machines had landed, the wheels had made big puddles on the surface of the field. Wigeon came in from the Tay to feed on this field and all night long they splashed and fed around the flashes. Other geese used this landing-ground and sometimes when a machine landed at night the birds had a bad scare. Manka was nearly cut down by a huge Whitley bomber that dropped silently in among a feeding gaggle. The first intimation the geese had of its arrival was the swish of wind through the strutting wires and a deafening burst from its engines. The geese fled in all directions and Manka was nearly struck by the outside edge of one of the huge wings.

It is strange how adaptable are geese, indeed this applies to all wildfowl. In the early days, before they became used to aeroplanes, the mere sound of one in the distance would send every goose on the Tay clamouring skywards. But in the last few years wildfowl have come to recognize flying machines as neutral and in the vicinity of an aerodrome they become quite fearless.

The following spring Comfrey died and the farm at Willowhills was empty. Mrs. Comfrey gave the geese away, Grey Mantle was given to Foxy.

"Take care of the poor thing," said Mrs. Comfrey. "My Frank was always so fond of his geese and I know he'd have liked you to have one."

"I'll look after 'er as though she were me own child, Mrs. Comfrey, I've just the place for 'er alongside me 'ens."

When Foxy got back to the cottage he took Grey Mantle behind the shed. Grey Mantle was fat, as fat as a farmyard goose, for the Comfreys had fed her well.

She struggled when she felt Foxy's hands about her neck. He killed her by the simple method of taking her by the head and whirling her body round and round.

Actually this is the most humane method of killing a goose, and death is instantaneous.

At that moment Manka was heading for Spitzbergen with no thought for poor Grey Mantle.

Four successive springs whitened the blossom of the apple trees at Willowhills, and later, red-cheeked apples dropped to the grass in the waspy days of August, for the farm remained without a tenant. The farm buildings were silent, save for the chirp of sparrows and the whistle of starlings, the pen where Manka had once been held a prisoner rotted away, only the upright posts remained and a few strands of rusty wire. Foxy had stolen most of the netting for his fowl-run, he also helped himself to the apples.

Four winter snows whitened those wide lands and in all that time Foxy only had three other chances at Manka, though the white goose came every year. One chance came in fog when the geese were lost, even Manka's sharp eyes could not distinguish the sinister figure crouching in a dyke. By a merciful chance the cartridge missed fire, for Foxy's aim had been true, and as he saw the white form swallowed in the mist he surely must have guessed

"The merciless sea"

there was something uncanny about Manka. Yet Foxy was dogged in his belief that one day, in his own time, he would kill the white goose.

On one of Manka's journeys from Spitzbergen he was forced down into the sea by wild weather. That had been a dolorous journey, the weather was all against the geese, and they met head-winds of almost gale force all the way. Big birds find it hard to battle against wind, for their wings are so large and have so wide a span. Manka came down the wrong side of Bear Island and half contemplated turning back. Night was coming on, the west was pale and each succeeding wave caught the dying rays.

The merciless sea! How terrible it is to reasoning beings. Manka did not feel the horror that man sometimes feels at the loneliness of the sea. Even sailors, whose life is spent upon it, occasionally have a glimpse of this horror, of blind forces that take no account of life.

Manka rested on the swell, rising gracefully to each roller, the dying light shining on his breast. He let himself drift, for his wings were deadly tired and he could not bring himself to rise into the air and continue the battle.

He drifted, like the black bottle which bobbed past him. Manka watched that drifting rubbish of the sea. It was a homely bottle tossed overboard from a liner . . . even a bottle seems to have a destiny.

With resting, Manka gained strength and took wing once more under cover of dark. The gale was dying, and flying was easier, though he had to rest again on the sea after a few hundred miles. A ship passed him fifty yards astern, every porthole gleaming. Manka saw figures moving on her decks and a motionless figure leaning over a rail. He did not understand what this monster could be, glaring at him from its many eyes, after a while it throbbed its way out of his ken.

Within three days he was back on the Tay with the rest of the geese and there rejoined his mate who had been restless at his absence. By mid-January he was back to the old life on the well-loved fields about the Grampians, listening once more to the voice of the Inchgarvie burn talking under the alders.

Moonlight nights on wild pastures, frosty dawns and sunny days, and for a background there was always the sea, the wild goose's greatest friend. There only was security and peace from Man. From his earliest beginnings Manka had been indebted to the sea, its music was part of his life; it was the sea that would give him peace at the long last. For Manka was an old goose now. Each journey to the Arctic tried him, the ancient road across the skies seemed longer. Yet the urge for adventure was still there, his wings had not yet finished their task, though they had borne him many thousands of miles and they would bear him many more.

No other living creature travels so far, or covers so much ground, as a migratory bird. Their lives are more full of variation than any living thing, change to a bird is a vital part of its existence. To deprive a wild bird of flight is to strike half its life away.

Chapter Thirteen
FOXY'S EYE

Moonlight nights on wild pastures, frosty dawns and sunny days, and for a background there was always the sea, the wild goose's greatest friend. There only was security and peace from man. From his earliest beginnings Manka had been indebted to the sea, its music was part of his life; it was the sea that would give him peace at long last.

On the first day, and the sun's warm light in the
Land sun's warm . . . in long . . . in their . . . in the
of Wicklow green. He flew up over a wall and out through
the grass he would . . . them clearly and . . . out . . . once
might get a chance to . . . down on them . . . the hawk
. . .

He sat hunched slightly forward in the . . . the . . . and swung
behind him . . . he old rock in the seat of the boat . . . held . . . on he

FOXY was getting rheumaticky. He did not take his punt out on the tideways so frequently. Years of exposure to wet and cold were beginning to tell and he was becoming an old man. He found he could no longer spring across the deep, winding gullies with the agility and ease of former years, and he walked with a slight limp.

One afternoon, two years after Grey Mantle's death, he set out in his punt from the little wooden stage by the mill. He paddled down the long, winding creek until he could see the wide expanse of the Wash, and the patches of white (which were flocks of resting gulls) on the sandbanks. The weather was fine and calm but very cold, and as he got out into the mid-channel he could see the snow lying on the flat fields inland.

Geese had been about all day, frozen off the young wheat, and soon Foxy saw a long line of them sitting on the sea off Mudhorse creek. There were over a mile away, but through his glasses he could focus them clearly and he thought there might be a chance to drift down on them with the flowing tide.

He sat, hunched slightly forward in the punt, his spaniel sitting behind him on an old sack in the stern of the boat. Before long he ceased paddling and lay down full length, guiding the craft with deft strokes of his hand-paddle over the side.

Above Boston Stump the sky was hazy and golden, the sun was westering, becoming redder and less dazzling every moment as it settled slowly into the haze. As is usual in still, frosty weather, sounds carried a long distance, and from the land he could hear a labourer singing at his work, the barking of dogs, the clear tones of Maplode St. Mark's church striking three o'clock and a steamer hooting beyond Boston Deeps. And the air was full of the crying of gulls over the tide-line. The mingled sounds were like the scrapings of violins, thin and musical, softened by distance. He drifted slowly, and though it was so cold he felt almost sleepy.

As Foxy drifted nearer, he could see the geese in detail. They were stretched out in a long string, about five hundred birds. Some were walking out of the water on to the sands, marching with gravity and dignity, some sitting down on the dry banks, some preening and settling down to snooze, others wading about in the shallow water.

As yet his approach had been unnoticed and all the geese were unsuspicious. Inch by inch he crept nearer, always keeping the nose of the punt towards the birds. If he had shown the length of the boat they would have spotted him at once. And then, as the distance lessened, the geese began to flock together with upraised heads. Those on the banks ceased to preen and splash about in the shallows, they were all watching the small white lump that was bearing down upon them. When he was within two hundred yards, the goose on the extreme left of the line began to run along the sand, and in a moment all the geese took the air with a deafening roar, bursting into a babel of crying and flying low over the water so that Foxy could see their reflections and the disturbed ripples in the shallows. They swung out seawards, then wheeled. Foxy thought they must be going inland, but to his surprise, they went along the tide and in a moment the whole skein was hidden by the big bleached hump of sand off Mudhorse creek.

They had not been badly frightened, and there was just a chance they had settled farther down the coast.

Foxy stretched, and moved his feet among the straw at the bottom of the punt. He sat, bent over his paddles and drew a pipe from his pocket. He would give them time to settle down again, for the tide was still half an hour from full flood and with the gathering mists he might get a better chance.

The little dog stood up too and shook herself violently, beginning with her nose and finishing with a shudder of her tail. She whined.

"Lie down, you," growled Foxy, and puffed at his pipe. Over the sea the mist was thickening and high in the sky was a young moon, pale curled, like a willow leaf, lying on its back.

To his left he saw a pied regiment of shelduck feeding in the shallow water and beyond them a dusky line of dots that were revealed by the glasses to be oyster catchers.

Only half the sun was visible now as it sank into the bank of mist and with its going the world became very grey and chill. There was frost on the barrel of the long gun and Foxy's numb feet tingled.

The tide drifted him past the sandbank and revealed an open expanse of shore with not a bird in sight save three little knot, no bigger than pebbles, sitting on the edge of the saltings. It was a mystery where the geese had gone, for he would surely have seen them had they gone inland or out to sea.

Foxy was always alive to possibilities and he knew that farther down there was the mouth of a big creek where many years ago he had surprised a gaggle of geese and had killed eighteen at one discharge. There was just a chance, the merest chance, that the geese had settled in the mouth of that very creek. Foxy was taking no chances.

He lay down again and kept close inshore, as near the edge of the muds as he dared to go and where the water was deep enough to float the punt.

He was aware that a mist, a thick mist, was coming down

This very often happens in frosty weather on the coast and Foxy was glad for this sudden change.

The knot on the foreshore had seen the punt, for now he was only thirty yards distant, and after bobbing their heads like red-shanks, they rose and flew away.

And then Foxy heard a distant clamour, a well-loved and familiar sound. Geese! Twisting his head sideways he saw, out of the tail of his eye, a skein of a dozen or so pink-feet coming in from the fields. They would be going out beyond the targets, thought Foxy, for they had been on the fields way back inland and were full fed.

It was surprising then, when he saw them set their wings, and with a great clamour swerve downwards and vanish beyond the lip of the high marsh. And there came an answering clamour. The geese were in the mouth of the gully sure enough.

In an instant Foxy's spirits began to rise. The disappointing afternoon was suddenly rosy with high hope and his pulses began to beat in his temples.

His right hand stole up to the lanyard of the gun and with his left he kept the craft close inshore. Soon he could hear the babel of talking geese. There must be the whole pack of them sitting in the gully mouth. What a chance!

Even as he drifted he saw more geese, as another line came swinging in. Those already massed behind the bank called them, and Foxy saw the long line slanting down. Then his heart beat quicker than before because he saw a white form lying third in the line. Manka!

All now were down and the thumping in Foxy's temples almost affected his sight. Even after years of fowling, excitement was as fresh as ever, it might have been his first shot.

Every moment the mist was thickening. Already Boston Stump had gone, a white wall was in its place, and the marsh close at hand was a mere blur. Only another eighty yards and he would be round the spit of sand and then. . . . But many things can happen, even in the last moment, perhaps a curlew was sitting just on the bend, or some sneaking redshank would betray him to the host.

An uncanny silence fell, even the geese were still and not a curlew called or a plover sounded.

Inch by inch he crept on towards the bend. Then he heard the murmur of geese, talking as geese talk with one another when they think they are alone. Bump! Bump! went Foxy's heart, his feet were tingling warm now and he could feel the spaniel shivering with excitement against his leg, for the dog could hear the geese much better than Foxy, and could smell them too.

In its excitement it gave a tiny whimper and Foxy kicked out savagely with his sea-boot. My God, if the dog put up the geese now he'd kill her!

The nose of the boat came round the point, ever so slowly but ever so surely, like a sinister, half-submerged crocodile.

Then Foxy saw the whole mouth of the bay was a mass of geese. In a flash he also saw Manka, dead in line with the muzzle of the big gun. They were not fifty yards away and, strange to say, not a goose had seen the punt.

Manka was preening. As the punt came round the bend he was stretching his broad wing over an extended paddle, like a big white fan.

Foxy thought quickly. If he put the geese up he would shoot more birds, but might miss Manka as he jumped. He would fire . . . NOW! His hand pulled the lanyard. . . . Then Foxy's world went out in a great blaze of red stars, then came blackness in which he felt his jaw working as though it did not belong to him, as though it were numbed with cocaine.

The blackness and the numbness grew and closed in on him from all sides. Somewhere in his brain a spark of consciousness still glowed, but it was slowly extinguished, though he fought hard against that snuffing out of light and life.

After what seemed just nothing, though he was aware deep down inside him that it *was* nothing, Foxy saw a greyish window open in his brain and then a tiny point of light like a little lamp, far, far away.

Quite suddenly he was fully conscious. He saw the point of light was a star. He lay still, staring upwards.

Then he moved his arm and felt his face. There was a warm wetness all down one side, it trickled over his hand and between his fingers. Perhaps the thermos that he carried in the punt had broken . . . what the devil was it all about . . . that star? He lay quite still, trying to collect his thoughts. Bit by bit the events of the afternoon came back to him. He remembered starting out from the staithe and the clock chiming three, the sunlight, the gulls. . . . Something was slapping, slapping the warm wetness of his face.

Foxy rolled over with a groan, then sat up. The spaniel was licking his face. He looked down at his hand. In the dusk it looked as though he wore a black glove. Then he saw it was blood. Sea water swilled on the bottom boards. He put his hand to his left eye, which was now beginning to drive a red-hot dagger right inside his head.

When he felt the socket he slumped back again to the bottom of the punt in a dead faint. His eye was not there.

Grey Mantle had been avenged. . . .

Will Wimble from Pingle Mill found Foxy on his way back from his fowling nets on the sands. It was low tide and full dawn. Will saw the long craft lying sideways on the bank and a whimpering dog running about the muds. Its pad-marks were everywhere, imprinted on the sand in a big circle, round and round the punt.

The barrel of the big gun was split open and one half was sticking up in the air like a twisted drain-pipe.

Inside the punt, lying partly on sand, was Foxy, horribly inert, soaked with water. But he was still alive.

That was how Foxy lost his eye. Had not Will found him that morning he would have "gone out."

But Foxy bore Will no gratitude and, as Will said afterwards, with an oath, "never so much as said thank you."

If Foxy had been unlovely in the sight of men before he lost his eye, he was a monster now. He did not even trouble to wear a patch over the gaping socket save when he wanted summer work from a farmer, or when he had something to sell.

The village children withdrew indoors when they saw him coming down the street to do his weekly shopping, and some of the bolder boys shouted uncomplimentary things in his effluvious wake.

"Old Foxy'll 'ave you," the women used to say to erring offspring. "'E'll take you into 'is cottage on the bank and scoop the liver out of you."

The ambition of his life, the death of Manka, ruled his days from October until March.

And every winter Manka came, quite oblivious, serenely so, of his formidable opponent. Always, for weeks at a time, he haunted the Wash marshes, and whenever the weather was open he came back to the rich feeding-lands about Mellons Platt.

The fowlers of the Suffolk coast knew him also, and looked for him, the Tollesbury gunners knew him and thirsted for his skin. The Severn gunners knew him, and even as far as Nigg and Cromarty he was known and hunted. But none looked so keenly, or worked so hard, as one-eyed Foxy, for none had so heavy a score to pay.

In his own time, somewhere, somehow, the day of reckoning should come.

"I'll die in peace then," thought Foxy, "even if I blow me head off, I'll shoot the —." And then Foxy would feel a creep of fear he could never understand. Perhaps he sensed that the white bird was somehow connected with his own destiny, that it was protected by some power he could not comprehend. Country people, especially those who live in remote districts, are prone to believe in witchcraft and devilment. The peasantry of Suffolk, for instance, are perhaps the most superstitious in England. It would be true to say he almost feared Manka.

Of course the good-natured raillery of the bar parlour of the Black Swan did not help matters, especially when Foxy was inflamed with drink. "'Sno good, Foxy, old White Goose'll be the finish of you." "You look out; that goose ain't no ornary goose, Foxy, it's one o' them bewitched buds you can't never shoot, not ef you used a machine-gun. It's bewitched, that's what it is. You let un be, Foxy, you let un be."

And then Foxy would jump his feet, dribbling with rage, the yellow fang of a tooth showing savagely.

"Lot o' old wimmin, that's what you are, that bud's no more bewitched than my sow. I'll get 'im I tell ye, in me own time and in me own way, you see!"

And with that he would stump out of the bar, back to the cottage on the sea-bank, spitting and cursing all the way.

Foxy had fallen foul of the new owner of Willowhills; the farmer would not have him near the place. He had caught Foxy on his land with a hare and a pheasant in his pocket, and as Foxy was now far past running the farmer had no difficulty in coming up with him. Foxy had gone to ground in a reedy dyke but was seen and ignominiously sent packing with the threat that if he ever set foot on the farm again he would be "run in."

Foxy by moonlight

The farmer never shot the land himself and this made Foxy all the more furious. On dark nights or in coarse weather he poached Willowhills with an even greater zest than before. But in the hours of daylight he dare not go near the farm and had to watch Manka and his comrades feeding with quite brazen impudence close to the orchard and sometimes almost within gunshot of the road. The farmer soon got to know Manka and look for him, he even went to the length of putting down old potatoes for the geese. With this new friendliness Manka used to come close to the farm where he had spent many months of captivity.

One day in the new year Foxy, passing along the road, saw the geese feeding close to the orchard and Manka was among them. He remembered how Manka, when in captivity, used to be fond of bread, and within his mind was suddenly born a hideous scheme.

That afternoon he got on his rusty bicycle and went to Fossfen, the nearest market town, and there went to see a friend of his, who kept a little hairdressing business in a back street. He was also a "fence" for Foxy's ill-gotten gains in the way of game.

Foxy opened the door of the little shop and went inside. There were no customers in the saloon, for it was the slack time of day, and Mr. Borrow was sitting by his fire with feet on the mantelpiece among the cracked shaving-cups and bottles of hair lotion.

"Well, Foxy, don't often see you 'ere this time o' year, no good bringing me any pheasants you know, not just now."

"Ain't pheasants I'm after, Mr. Borrer, it's fish-hooks—eel 'ooks. Got any?"

"Why, going fishin'?" queried Borrow, rummaging in a drawer and producing a bundle of big galvanized hooks.

"Ah, thought o' doin' a bit in the middle drain, there's some rare big eels there."

"'Ow many d'you want?"

"Oh, two pennoth, Mr. Borrer, two pennoth'll do."

That night, before the moon rose, Foxy went up to the orchard and under cover of darkness laid his horrible implements of death.

To each hook he fastened a length of fine wire, tying it to the fence. And on each hook he put a large lump of white bread, burying the barb up beyond the hilt. If any geese came they would no doubt swallow the bread and be held fast until Foxy could get to them and wring their necks.

After laying as many as a dozen lines he slunk back to the shelter of the orchard and got down into a ditch. In a short time the moon began to come up over Mellons Platt and throw shadows from the bare orchard trees. Above Foxy's head was an old gold-finch's nest, like a little golf ball fixed in the end of a pruned branch, just where the new growth sprouted. It was amazing how nests seemed to stand the winter winds, especially the wild winds of the coast.

In the moonlight Foxy could see one of the little white lumps of bread on the stubble, it looked like a scrap of white paper. Like all frosty nights it was deathly still, and he could hear cars passing along the Boston road and merry singing from the bar of the Black Swan.

The hours went by, but still the geese did not come. He heard other parties going out over the land, but they were very far away. The moon rose higher in the sky until it threw an interlacing shadow from the bare apple boughs on the stubble in front of Foxy's hide.

Then a car came along the lane, dimming the moonlight. It swung round, the headlamps glare passing like a searchlight beam across the field, and Foxy crouched down. The farmer had come home. He heard him opening the door of the garage and switching off the engine. Then his steps went across the cobbled yard to the back door. A dog started to bark. It barked until someone came out of the house and let it off the chain.

Foxy swore, for he knew the dog, a half-bred greyhound which had nipped Foxy once in the seat of his trousers. If he ever met it along the sea-wall, he'd shoot it, if there was no one about.

All was quiet again then and a large rat rustled up the ditch. He heard louder singing from the direction of the village, and men talking to one another. Though the inn was some distance from Willowhills farm he heard somebody shout, "Good night, Ernie, make it up wi' the missus!" followed by a roar of laughter. It must be closing time.

Then he heard the single call of a goose from over the field, and before Foxy would say "knife" the air was full of big shapes planing down. Right over his head they came, pitching in the middle of the field. If Foxy had dared to carry a gun he could have had a glorious right and left as they passed over the apple tree.

And there, in the moonlight, was Manka, silver in the greenish light with a dark pool of shadow behind him. Foxy had never been so close to Manka since the day he had him in his hands, years before.

He was only a dozen yards distant and standing very still. Then he began to eat the scraps of bread that Foxy had scattered about the baited hooks.

Now and again he would stop and look around him. Perhaps his guardian angel warned him all was not well. Other geese came over and joined Manka, but they did not touch the bread. Another foot or two and Manka would be right among the baited lines.

Then, for no apparent reason, Manka sprang into the air, and all the other geese followed suit. Foxy heard them going away towards the sea-wall and after a while the crying died to silence. What could have disturbed them? Foxy could have wept aloud; just when triumph seemed in his grasp he had been robbed of victory. And then Foxy saw something moving in the moonlight twenty yards away. It was the lurcher dog. And it was eating the pieces of bread! It moved slinkily from one crust to another, gulping them down.

Foxy was so flabbergasted he did not know what to do. If the dog swallowed a baited hook there would be hell to pay. If he disturbed the dog it would rouse the whole farm.

But his indecision was arrested by a sudden scream of agony from the dog which in a moment was writhing on the ground. The noise was frightful. The stout wire held for a moment, then parted with a twang, and the dog fled tow-rowing towards the farm. Doors opened. Angry voices called.

Foxy, lame with rheumatism, could not run fast. Anyway, it would be bad policy, a man running in heavy boots makes a good deal of noise.

Foxy slunk down the ditch, like his namesake, and went back to the cottage on the bank.

There was a great deal of noise about the dog. His master took it to the vet. and had the hook cut out. He also made inquiries.

Five days afterwards, Foxy had a nasty shock when he saw a blue helmet sliding along the privet hedge that led to his cottage.

The sergeant propelled himself up to Foxy's door, carefully leaning his bicycle against the gate. Foxy looked out of his single eye with a sort of frozen horror.

"Mornin', sergeant, what d'you want o' me?"

The sergeant bent to adjust a trouser clip and Foxy saw the well-fed, beefy neck, pink with scrubbing. He came up to Foxy slowly. His eyes were unfriendly and he did not answer Foxy's greeting. He put one finger in his pocket and produced a bent and blood-stained eel hook.

"That's not yours, be any chance?"

Foxy took it, peering at it closely, and turning it over and over on his dirty palm. Foxy shook his head slowly from side to side.

"Never 'ave call to use sich things."

"'Aven't bought any lately, I suppose?"

Again Foxy shook his head.

"No. What should I want wi' a 'ook like that? I'm a gunner, not a fisher."

The sergeant ran his finger round his chin-strap.

"Supposin' I told you you'd bought two pennoth in Fossfen last week, what d'you say?"

Foxy suddenly seemed to affect a great surprise.

"Why, bless you, yes. Now I come to think on it, I *did* buy two pennoth at Borrer's shop. There was some eels I wanted to catch."

"Funny time o' year to cotch eels, ain't it?"

Foxy tried to laugh.

"No, I fish for 'em all times in the drains."

"Suppose you couldn't be showin' me the 'ooks you bought, could you?"

"Well, no, dunno quite where I put 'em now."

Foxy scratched his head. Things were getting a bit warm.

Then came the dreaded words.

"What did you set them fish-hooks up at Willow'ills for last week, don't you know you caught Mr. Winnan's dog?"

"I never set no lines at Willow'ills, sergeant, why should I do that, there ain't no eels on the big medder."

The sergeant looked Foxy in the eye.

"It's no good, Foxy. I knows you set 'em there. Mr. Winnan's reported it to the S.P.C.A. I shall 'ave to make my report."

The sergeant's two fingers were inserted into his breast pocket. He withdrew a fat little note-book encircled by a rubber band.

He wet the stump of a pencil and began to make laborious notes, resting the note-book on Foxy's gate-post.

The result was that Foxy was absent from the cottage and his red-eyed little wife for a month. The magistrate was severe. He and Foxy had met before. "A brutal practice" was the verdict.

And while Foxy was enjoying a short change in his mode of

living, at the expense of His Majesty, Manka, the cause of all the trouble, went away North to Cromarty, also for a change, and by some queer twist of ironical chance came back the day after Foxy returned, with only a week to go to the end of the fowling season. So the destinies of both man and bird seemed indeed united.

Perhaps in some past existence Foxy and Manka had been enemies, some people have theories of that kind. Both were approaching the final drama, the end of a story thirty years long.

Chapter Fourteen

THE LAST CHAPTER

Manka held straight, straight as a die for the big banks. He was taking a chance and he knew it. To-morrow they would be off! Spitzbergen, the Esker bluffs! The never-setting sun! . . . the pain to be gone was strong, he sensed the coming thaw.

THE long twilights had come again and the aeroplanes were back on the bombing ranges, making the days hideous with buzzings and bangings. They swept above the marshes with stuttering machine-guns and the red flag flew from the pole on the bank, warning trespassers to keep away.

To Manka and his mate had come the wander pain once more. Already, maybe, they saw in their minds the white-clad peaks and icy glaciers around Sassen Bay and, most impelling of all, the bluffs and breeding-ledges of the Esker river.

Had the weather remained open they would have gone North to the Tay, where thousands of other geese were assembling, but in the last week of February a short snap set in, and the geese dallied. There was little frost, but it snowed fitfully and the air was bitterly cold.

Out of a dun-coloured sky stray flakes wandered, lonesome and large, thickening soon to a moving curtain that blotted out the marshes and the sea. Moithered by the flakes the geese flew low about the sea-wall, for they hated falling snow as much as fog.

Three rooks were sitting in a baby oak tree that grew in the hedge behind Mellons Platt, not far from the sea-wall. The rich dark earth was mantled in white, and they had sat thus for over an hour, croaking dismally one to another. It was an unexpected change, for only a week before they had been thinking about household duties in the rookery by the farm. Now winter had come back and hopes were dashed. They sat puffed out, with raised crests, watching the wavering flakes blot out the distant dark line of trees by Mellons Platt.

And then one of them drew itself up and depressed its feathers for it had seen a figure coming along the sea-bank. It croaked an alarm and all three flew leisurely away, to be hidden, in a very few moments, by the driving snow.

Foxy, with collar turned up, was tramping along with bent head, the front of his coat whitened by the blizzard. It was a splendid day, from Foxy's point of view; he might get a shot at a pheasant under cover of the snow.

A hare was crouched, like a clod of earth, beside a gateway. The snow had whitened it and Foxy did not see it until he was on the bank above. Then the hare stretched its legs and made off under the gate. Up came Foxy's gun; for a split second his single rheumy eye squinted down the barrel, then a puff of smoke jetted. The hare rolled over, kicking in the snow, and Foxy darted down the bank, jumped the drain (slipping in and wetting his leg to the thigh) and quickly thrust the limp brown body into his capacious bag. Then he climbed back over the drain and continued his walk down the sea-wall.

When he got to the shepherd's hut he struck out across the marshes, heading for Horseshoe Gull. There was a lively chance of a duck on such an afternoon and he might have some luck on this, the last day of the season.

On Leader's Drove the geese had been feeding all morning, scraping away the snow to get at the tender blades of wheat. The snow was criss-crossed in every direction by their paddle-prints and greeny-white droppings were everywhere.

Manka and his mate were with them; in the snow all looked alike, all appeared to be albino birds, for the flakes settled on their plumage. Late in the afternoon they rose from the field and went away for the marshes.

The snow had ceased, and over the sea was a clear patch of sky of the faintest prussian blue. Mild weather was coming, and the next day the geese would be away for the Tay, and very soon the journey would begin, the long journey to Spitzbergen.

As usual, Manka headed the skein, and with a great clamour they held their course straight over the shepherd's hut.

The guardian angel that had watched over Manka for thirty years may have lost patience. Perhaps by the law of averages there was bound to come a day of destiny for Manka.

That he had managed to survive for so long a time was wonderful, for he was doubly handicapped by the fact of his white plumage. How strange it is that man should desire to kill a creature just because it is rare!

If we could have drawn a chart of Manka's life and compared it with one of Foxy's, how different they would have been! Manka had seen so much and had travelled widely; Foxy had never been farther afield than Boston. He had never even given a thought to that far land across the sea, to the snow-clad hills of Scotland, to the wonders of a wild bird's life. He was content to remain in his own little well-trodden locality, as content as a cow chewing the cud in a field. His life had been the meaner, full of cruelty and selfishness, blind even to the beauties of the marshes and the glory of dawn or sunset. With all his vonderful superiority of brain (I will not say intellect) he had never exercised his intelligence, his only delight was to destroy, to eat, to drink, to sleep.

As he spread out the sack which he carried in his bag (warm now from the hare's body) a break slowly appeared in the snow clouds over Boston, and the sun burst through, sending down long silver bars that lit the water and transformed the muds. It shone full upon him and threw a shadow on the tangled sea-lavender, where the tide had begun to turn back on its ageless journey to the sea. Foxy idly looked at the water. The "old man" was going out again. Foxy had had many escapes from the "old man." A slimy, merciless enemy, who slipped up behind one on the marshes and was always scheming to trap the unwary. Well it had never trapped Foxy, and it wouldn't get the chance.

He remembered once how he had got stuck in some soft creek mud up Frieston way. It was a long time ago now, when he was a young man. Even as he thought of it a shiver went down his spine. It had been a near go, the "old man" had nearly had him then. Unused in those days to the ways of mud and quicksands, he had panicked, instead of lying down in the stuff and rolling out. There is no quicksand in the world that you cannot get out of if you keep your head. Foxy had struggled and finally screamed, a horrible sound, but only the gulls had mocked him. Those big black gulls, how he hated them, always laughing at him, stealing his wounded birds, giving him away. The tide had crept in, he had seen it coming slowly, white-lipped and rustling, with a sinister sureness that nearly drove him out of his mind.

But a man working on the sea-wall had heard him and had pulled him out, a sobered and very frightened Foxy. Ugh! that had been a near go. Sometimes when he was alone at night, far out on the outmarsh, he had been gripped by a feeling of panic and had run back to the bank. In foggy weather too, before he had come to know these marshes, that now he could walk blind-fold, he had had some narrow squeaks. That time in Horseshoe creek. . . . Foxy thought of other things.

A redshank came up the creek. It did not see Foxy crouching under the rim of the bank. It lit on the edge of the mud and bobbed its head, making a plaintive, piping noise. Then it began to run daintily along, its bright orange legs twinkling as it probed the muds.

Foxy wondered where Manka had got to. He knew the geese were in the district, for that morning he had seen them on Leader's

Drove, appearing on the snow like enormous wood-pigeons. Manka had been right on the far side of the field, he had seen him through his glasses.

Damn the bird! He almost wished some shore-popper would shoot him. Since the episode of the fish-hooks, the tale had gone all over the district and he was a laughing-stock. He'd show 'em. He'd shoot Manka one of these days and walk into the Black Swan and throw the white body on the floor and affect great boredom and superiority.

He looked landwards. A tiny figure was passing along the bank. It was Billy going to visit the lambing-fold beyond the main drain bank. There was a collection of hurdles there thatched with straw, and it had been a big "fall" this year, the pens were full of unsteady-legged, bleating lambs.

He watched the pygmy figure moving ever so slowly along the ridge of the sea-wall till it disappeared over the bank. Billy had changed, he was not friendly as he used to be. Well . . . damn them all, Foxy would live his own life and they could live theirs, the whole boiling of them. Foxy spat into the drain and watched, with his single eye, the little spot of white, as big as a sixpence, slowly drift away towards the sea.

Glug! glug! gulped the mud walls of the creek. He could see the tide dropping and hear the tiny channels that fed the main drain begin to gush water.

There was a big cloud near the sinking sun. It was edged with a lace of bright burning gold. Flocks of waders passed up the shore like smoke; "little buds" as Foxy called them.

Come to-morrow and the season would be over. No more shooting for six months. It would be difficult to get work this summer with the farmers, he'd set their backs up with his poaching and stealing, and now, with this last affair, he'd have to go farther afield to earn a few shillings. Well, he didn't care, he'd saved a bit, quite a tidy bit, and his wife worked for the Shardwaners now, she'd be getting something extra for the spring cleaning.

And then Foxy squatted like a partridge, for he suddenly heard the clamouring of the geese, that lovely song that is the voice of the land where no man comes.

Yes . . . there they were, and my God, they were coming low from the fields! Yes . . . and there was Manka right in the lead! Foxy rolled up tight, one eye watering with excitement, mouth open. Would they change their line, was there another gun somewhere up a creek who would fire and scare them off? "Damn!" swore Foxy, they were going too much to the right. But no, he saw Manka swerve and turn. Billy was there with his sheep. Yes, they were heading now straight for Horseshoe gully. Foxy's big scarred thumb went up and the hammer of his big eight-bore clicked back, click! for safety, click! again for full-cock.

Here they came, wavering a little up and down, not forty yards high. Thought they were safe, did they? That white —— in front was going to make his last mistake. Foxy remembered his eye, the fish-hooks, the soaking clothes, the muddy crawls he had had after Manka. Let him come on, that's all; let him come on. He'd get drunk to-night. God! supposing he missed! The last day, too; might be his last chance. If he missed now there was all that weary waiting, the gibes of his enemies, the long days of summer.

Manka held straight, straight as a die, for the big banks. He was taking a chance and he knew it. To-morrow they would be off! Spitzbergen, the Esker bluffs! The never-setting sun!

Did Manka think of those things? Or did he only seek rest on the sandbanks? The pain to be gone was strong, he sensed the coming thaw.

"Anka!" he called, and his mate answered. She was flying close behind. . . .

Manka did not see Foxy until the latter rose from the gully, not hastily, but with deadly calm. He saw the sudden movement

Three rooks sitting in the snow

of the gun barrel, and flung himself up with quick-beating wing, crying the alarm.

For a second he climbed. In that short time he drove up eight feet with his broad white wings.

The recoil from Foxy's gun was terrific. The cartridge had been damp and it was a very old one, bought in Boston six years before.

He staggered and nearly fell into the drain, in his nostrils was the keen reek of the powder.

He swore a dreadful oath, for Manka did not fall. Foxy stood, with smoking gun in his hands, then with a violent spasm of anger hurled it down on the crab grass.

All the geese had ceased to call to one another when they saw Foxy, for exertion had been concentrated in climbing. Now they broke out again, a great clamour.

Manka was higher than the rest and still climbing, and Foxy shaded his eye with a grimy claw.

"By God! He's 'it!" said Foxy. "'Es towerin' like a partridge. I've got 'im at last!"

Manka continued to climb, straight up and up like a lark. For a moment or two he was against a dark snow-cloud, and still he rose.

The rest of the skein went on towards the sea, already they were out of sight. Foxy's eye was on the white form that still climbed heavenwards. Quickly he bent and felt for his gun, his eye still on the goose.

Higher still, off the dark snow cloud now, and grey against the thin-washed blue of clear sky, the sunset shining on him until he was as pink as a flamingo. Like Icarus he rose into the burning gold so that Foxy's eye was dazzled.

And then he saw a spot of white, falling as a stone falls.
"HE'S DOWN!" . . .

The man ran, and the spaniel ran, the former stumbling into gullies and once falling headlong on his face.

The dog went on ahead and disappeared over the edge of a creek. When Foxy came up he realized two things. One, that Manka had fallen in the outlet of a deep dyke; secondly, that from his lower level, the dog could not see the white body drifting slowly down the middle of the drain. The spaniel was splattering about on the margin of the mud, trying up creek instead of down. There was not a moment to lose.

Foxy knew this creek well. Thirty yards farther on it hooked to the left, almost in a hairpin bend, and then went straight out into the Wash. It was at all points too deep to wade, even at low water. His only hope was to run beyond the outmarsh on to the muds, and try and get Manka as he drifted past the sand bar, or to trust that the dog would see the goose and fetch it in. The wayward little beast was a long way up the creek, and Foxy roared with rage until a dribble ran out of his mouth and glistened among the stubbly red hairs of his chin. But the dog was too far away to hear him. Always a wild creature and unbiddable, it had spied a dead curlew that was lying on the far side of the creek. Foxy saw it plunge in and swim across. It picked up the curlew and came back, bringing the bird to Foxy in triumph, with wagging stump.

Meanwhile, the white, motionless body drifted away round the bend, straight for the open sea.

Then Foxy lost control of himself. His face flushed red with passion. He raised the gun and shot his dog. It slithered down the bank and rolled into the drain.

Foxy turned about and ran for the outmuds. As he ran he gasped and groaned. Damn the dog, served him right, never had been any good. He'd get the white goose if he had to swim for it. Now, with hard running, he was almost abreast of Manka's body. All he could see was the half-submerged breast and two wings sticking like sails out of the water. The stream was sliding out fast, but Foxy could run faster and he was at the bar, waiting, when Manka's body came round the bend.

Foxy saw it would pass within five yards of where he stood and he plunged in. The water was deeper than he thought. In five steps it was over his waders, and he felt its icy chill. With luck he could just reach Manka with his gun-barrel. He stretched out and touched one white wing. The inert body swung round, paused a moment and then . . . the current gently wheeled it outwards. Foxy reached out farther, took a step forward and lost his balance. The gun slipped from his hand, and with a gasp, the marshes, the setting sun, the distant finger of Boston Stump, vanished in a yellow choking darkness, that filled eye, ears, and lungs. Foxy bubbled like a bottle, a frightened crab scuttled.

The "old man" had got him at last and was not going to let him go. The tide tucked him under his arm and took him out towards the sea that is the mother of all the waters of the world. . . .

Billy, having finished his work with the sheep, came up the bank and started to walk home.

The sun had gone and had left the marshes grey, a little breeze was thrumming in the telegraph wires overhead.

Out over the sea night was coming and far away, beyond the tide-line, a cloud of white gulls was stooping and calling at something in the water. They were making such a clamour that Billy stopped. What could it be, a shoal of fish? . . . a porpoise, perhaps. . . .

On the little bent apple tree in his garden he heard a song thrush singing, and from the bottom of a tarred rail of the stile a line of drops like pearls were hung all a row. Yes, the thaw was coming right enough, it would be grand for the lambing. Once again he looked seawards and saw the gulls were scattering. From Boston a line of stars winked and jumped against the clouds of coming night.

The tide was still running out. . . . Foxy and Manka went out on the tide.

THE END

A FLUTE IN MAYFERRY STREET

Eileen Dunlop ISBN 0 86267 183 3

Edinburgh's new Town is the city's beautiful late eighteenth-century quarter, and a tall quiet but somewhat sad house in one of its shabbier streets is the setting for this second novel by Eileen Dunlop. Here live three members of the once prosperous Ramsay family, and when we first meet them, none of them is very content with daily life. Mrs Ramsay wonders how she can make ends meet. Marion feels her existence appallingly restricted by ill-health, and Colin pines for something he can never, he thinks, have — a flute of his own.

Award winning author, Eileen Dunlop was born at Alloa, and educated in Alloa and Edinburgh. She has worked with children all her life and is currently Head of the Preparatory School of Dollar Academy. Her novels which have won high acclaim include *Robinsheugh (Swallow)*, *Fox Farm*, *The Maze Stone*, *Clementina*, and *The House on the Hill.*

ROBINSHEUGH

Eileen Dunlop   ISBN 0 86267 194 9

Robinsheugh stands in the Scottish Border Country, a region where the line between the past and the present seems curiously indefinite. Elizabeth Martin is sent there to spend a summer with an aunt who seems more concerned with Robinsheugh's eighteenth-century owners that with her own niece, though a few years back the two of them had enjoyed a warm friendship. To Elizabeth, desperately lonely, unsure of herself and of others, the old house itself offers a strange alternative to misery — but one for which a harsh price has to be paid.

'It is dominated by the theme of the historical imagination and its power under certain circumstances to eclipse the present entirely . . . an impressive first book.'

The Times Literary Supplement

SWALLOW BOOKS

SWALLOW PAPERBACKS
  —the current list
  —A FLUTE IN MAYFERRY STREET
  Eileen Dunlop

  —THE LAST HARPER
  Julian Atterton

  —THE WAR ORPHAN
  Rachel Anderson

  —THE WHITE NIGHTS OF ST PETERSBURG
  Geoffrey Trease

  —NO HERO FOR THE KAISER
  Rudolph Frank

  —THE YEAR OF THE STRANGER
  Allan Campbell McLean

  —ROBINSHEUGH
  Eileen Dunlop

  —THE SENTINELS
  Peter Carter

  —KING CREATURE COME
  John Rowe Townsend

  —THE RIVER TREE
  Mairi MacLachlan

  —THE TOURNAMENT OF FORTUNE
  Julian Atterton

  —MANKA THE SKY GIPSY
  'BB'

  —GIFTWISH
  Graham Dunstan Martin

  —THE THIRD EYE
  Mollie Hunter

  —TOMB OF REEDS
  Sarah Baylis

  —ON THE ISLAND
  Iain Crichton Smith

swallow